T. ANN'S CATHOLIC 1929

∧ SOUTH ABBOTSFORD MENNONITE BRETHREN 1932

EST ABBOTSFORD MENNONITE 1936   BETHEL REFORMED 1954 ∨

∧ ABBOTSFORD ALLIANCE 1948   FIRST CHRISTIAN REFORMED 1955 ∨

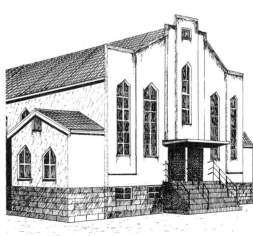

The Church
in the Heart
of the Valley

1892–1992

Edited by

A.J. KLASSEN

Matsqui–Abbotsford Ministerial Association
ABBOTSFORD, B.C.

DEDICATION

To the pioneers who founded the churches

and the volunteers who contributed their time and talent

to the building of these churches in

the heart of the Fraser Valley.

Credits:
Cover Photo: Matsqui Lutheran Church
Photos by: Participating Churches
               Matsqui-Sumas-Abbotsford News
               MSA Museum

CANADIAN CATALOGUING IN PUBLICATION DATA
Klassen, A. J., ed.
The Church in the Heart of the Valley:
ISBN 0-9693396-1-5
1. History of Churches, Matsqui–Abbotsford, B.C. — History
2. Churches, Christian, Fraser Valley, Abbotsford, B.C.
I. Title

Typesetting by Kehler & Company   Cover Design by David Ediger
Printed and bound in Canada by Abbotsford Printing

Contents

SECTION ONE:
The Churches in the Heart of the Valley

METHODIST

NAZARENE

PENTECOSTAL

PRESBYTERIAN

REFORMED

SEVENTH DAY ADVENTIST

UNITED CHURCH OF CANADA

INDEPENDENT

SECTION TWO:
Church-Related Institutions

SCHOOLS

RELIEF ORGANIZATIONS

SENIOR CITIZENS FACILITIES

Preface

The Church in the Heart of the Valley began with a request from the Matsqui Centennial Committee, inviting churches to participate in the celebration in a tangible way. In response, the Matsqui–Abbotsford Ministerial Association (MAMA) appointed a study committee to develop a proposal for a book that would highlight the history and role of the churches during the past 100 years.

Each church was invited to contribute a manuscript and pictures telling its own story and present ministry in the community. Church-related institutions which appeared on the scene during the last half century were included to reflect changes in our society and growth in the mission of the church.

Many individuals spent time locating appropriate photos and writing histories. By-lines have been included where the writers identified themselves.

The large number of churches in a relatively small area reflects the significance of the church in our society and has earned Matsqui–Abbotsford the reputation as the "Bible Belt" of B.C. The inside covers offer a historical overview as well as a comparative study in church architecture. The timeline provides a guide to a century of founding churches and institutions in the heart of the Fraser Valley. A select bibliography indicates additional resources for reading and study.

Many people contributed to the preparation of this manuscript. The MAMA adopted this as its centennial project and appointed the editor as well as a committee of readers consisting of Henry Wiebe (Alliance), Ron Beharrell (United Church), John Kampman (CRC) and Jake Tilitzky (Conference of Mennonites in B.C.). They provided helpful counsel, direction, guidance and critique.

A large number of the contributions were made on computer diskettes, which greatly facilitated the editing process. Betty Klassen, wife of the editor, assumed responsibility for keyboarding and copy editing. My heartfelt thanks to all who have made *The Church in the Heart of the Valley* possible.

"No individual or corporate history is complete without an understanding of our spiritual heritage," stated Lieutenant Governor David Lam at the Matsqui Centennial dinner on October 9, 1992. May this book contribute to that end.

A. J. KLASSEN, editor
All Saints Day, 1992

Foreword

With joy, the churches of the Fraser Valley join the people of the District of Matsqui in celebrating their Centennial with this special project — *The Church in the Heart of the Valley*. One of the truly unique features of this community is its rich, varied and strong Christian heritage. One cannot truthfully tell the history of Matsqui and the surrounding area without taking account of the influence of the church on the lives of the people who pioneered and developed it. While this is true for the history of our entire country, it is especially true for this particular region.

Consequently, a suggestion was made, and the Matsqui–Abbotsford Ministerial Association (MAMA) took up the challenge, of publishing this volume. Hundreds of people have been involved in bringing the project to fruition. We are grateful for the contribution of every local church pastor, history editor and governing body member involved. An extra special thanks goes to Dr. A. J. Klassen, who has been the driving force behind the book. Ultimately, he carried the ball from beginning to end and deserves the credit. Thank you, A. J! We also express appreciation to the Matsqui Centennial Committee and the sponsoring churches who invested the start-up capital necessary to make the project a reality.

As you read this volume, may you enjoy the history of people at work, play and worship. It is alive with the same excitement and adventure characteristic of our fast-moving society. May you grow in appreciation for the abundant heritage passed on to us and for the sacrifice of those who have gone before to make it possible. And as you read, breathe a prayer of thanks to God for "great things He has done!"

Rev. J. J. Ross Johnston, Chairman
Matsqui–Abbotsford Ministerial Association
Pastor, Abbotsford Church of the Nazarene

Abbreviations

Alliance	Christian & Missionary Alliance
BOCE	Board of Church Extension of the B.C. Conference of Mennonite Brethren Churches
CBC	Columbia Bible College
CGIT	Canadian Girls in Training (United Church)
CMinBC	Conference of Mennonites in B.C.
CRC	Christian Reformed Church
MAMA	Matsqui–Abbotsford Ministerial Association
MB	Mennonite Brethren
MBM/S	Mennonite Brethren Missions/Services
MCC	Mennonite Central Committee
MEI	Mennonite Educational Institute
SDA	Seventh Day Adventist
UCW	United Church Women
VCS	Valley Christian School
WPBC	Western Pentecostal Bible College

Timeline of Churches & Institutions

1880   Abbotsford Presbyterian/Trinity Memorial United
1892   Matsqui Lutheran
1894   Mt. Lehman Presbyterian/United
1900   St. Matthew's Anglican
1900   Bradner Presbyterian
1907   Calvin Presbyterian
1910   St. Ann's Catholic
1910   Matsqui/Abbotsford Baptist
1924   Church of the Nazarene
1925   Poplar United
1926   Abbotsford Pentecostal
1930   Trinity Lutheran
1932   South Abbotsford Mennonite Brethren
1934   Russian Orthodox Chapel of St. Peter & St. Paul
1936   Peace Lutheran
1936   West Abbotsford Mennonite
1936   North Abbotsford Mennonite Brethren/Clearbrook
1936   MB Bible School
1937   Bethel Bible School
1943   Arnold Mennonite Brethren
1943   Seventh Day Adventist
1944   Mennonite Educational Institute (MEI)
1945   Matsqui Mennonite Brethren
1946   Grace Evangelical Bible
1947   East Aldergrove Mennonite Brethren
1948   Abbotsford Alliance/Sevenoaks
1950   Church of God in Christ Mennonite
1950   Abbotsford Mennonite Brethren/Central Heights
1950   First Christian Reformed
1952   Clearbrook Mennonite
1953   Abbotsford Christian School
1954   Menno Home
1954   Bethel Reformed
1955   Prairie Chapel
1956   Abbotsford Christian Assembly
1958   Abbotsford Evangelical Free
1960   Menno Hospital
1960   Olivet Mennonite
1961   Tabor Home
1961   Canadian Reformed
1962   Western Pentecostal Bible College
1962   Gifford Chapel

1963	Ebenezer Mennonite
1964	Mennonite Central Committee (MCC B.C.)
1965	Bakerview Mennonite Brethren
1966	Peace Lutheran
1966	King Road Mennonite Brethren
1969	Second Christian Reformed
1972	Ebenezer Senior Home
1972	Community Baptist
1973	Maranatha Baptist
1975	Highland Mennonite Brethren Community
1975	Abbotsford Foursquare Gospel
1977	Trinity Christian Reformed
1978	Abbotsford Christian Academy
1979	Zion Christian Reformed
1979	Abbotsford Christian Senior Secondary School
1980	Family Worship Centre
1980	Emmanuel Mennonite
1980	Northview Mennonite Brethren Community
1980	Clearbrook Christian Centre
1981	Gladwin Heights United
1982	Emmanuel Full Gospel Fellowship
1983	Free Methodist/Cornerstone Community
1983	Laotian Christian
1984	Immanuel Baptist
1984	Cedar Park Christian Fellowship
1984	Covenant Fellowship
1984	Living Faith Christian Centre
1984	Salvation Army
1985	Central Valley Baptist
1985	St. Ann's Elementary School
1986	New Life Christian Reformed
1986	Abbotsford Christian Fellowship
1986	Valley Christian School
1986	Body of Christ Ministries
1987	Bakerview Hispanic Mennonite Brethren
1987	Abbotsford Spanish Fellowship
1988	Heritage Alliance
1988	St. Michael Anglican Catholic
1989	West Clearbrook Mennonite Brethren
1990	Abbotsford Chinese Christian
1991	Clearbrook Vietnamese
1991	Abbotsford Christian School — Clayburn Hills Campus
1991	Mountain Park Mennonite Brethren Community
1991	Christian Life Community

Introduction

This book has its setting in the heart of the Fraser Valley, bounded by the Fraser River on the north and the United States border on the south.

The first known people to live in this area were the Matsqui and Sumas bands of the Stalo Indians whose history goes back some 10,000 years.

The first Europeans to arrive were explorers, followed by fur traders who came as far as Fort Langley by the early nineteenth century. The Gold Rush of 1858 brought Scots, Irish, and Englishmen to the crown colony of British Columbia, established November 19, 1858.

The first known presence of the church in the area can be traced to the coming of the Oblate Fathers in 1840. They established St. Mary's Mission on the north bank of the Fraser, in 1862. The founding of an Indian residential school and the arrival of the Sisters of St. Ann led to the purchase of 1,200 acres of land in the Matsqui flats directly across the river to begin a model farming community.

The pictures of the first church buildings of various denominations described here are portrayed chronologically on the inside front cover. Some of the early churches pictured here were absorbed by larger congregations, closed, sold, demolished or restored at a later date.

The arrival of the Rev. Alexander Dunn from the Church of Scotland, served numerous preaching points in his Langley parish which was some 100 miles in length and from 10-30 miles in width. He was stationed here from 1875 to 1886 with preaching posts that included Upper Sumas, Matsqui and Mt. Lehman. The first Presbyterian Church of Abbotsford dates its beginning as 1880, though the first "little church on the hill" was completed under the guidance of Rev. John Charles Alder in 1908. Baptist, Methodist, Presbyterian and Anglican ministers rotated in conducting services in the school at Mt. Lehman which officially became a Presbyterian congregation in 1903.

Services for Lutherans of Scandanavian descent were conducted by circuit riders, who conducted the first baptism in 1892. The meeting to establish the Matsqui Lutheran congregation, however, occurred in 1903. The church building, begun in 1904, was completed in 1920. Trinity Lutheran began in 1930, while Peace Lutheran served the needs of German-speaking Lutherans from 1936 on.

On October 28, 1900, St. Matthew's Anglican Church, which seated

Pinegrove United Church

100 persons, was dedicated by Archbishop A. P. DePencier of New Westminster.

In 1902, Ruth and Ann Williams, devout Presbyterians, built a tiny chapel and began an interdenominational Sunday School in the Peardonville area. When the building was moved to the corner of Marshall Extension and Peardonville in the 1920's, it was renamed Pinegrove United Church following the union of 1925. Later, the group joined Trinity United.

Poplar United began in 1925 and a small church was erected at the intersection of King and Clearbrook roads. Eventually, the congregation was absorbed into the larger Trinity United Church. Since the property had originally been donated with the specification that it be used for church or church school purposes, it was sold to the King Road Mennonite Brethren Church in 1967 and later replaced by a new building.

Poplar United Church

The Pioneer Clayburn Church served its community from 1912 to 1958.

Photo: Pioneer Clayburn Church

7

After two decades of disuse, it was restored and now continues to serve its community.

Although the precise date of founding St. Ann's Roman Catholic Church is unclear, we have already noted the attempts of the Oblate Fathers to establish a Native farming community in Matsqui in the 1880's. Beginning in 1910, Catholic services were held in the spacious de la Giroday home, until a church was built. Then Mass was conducted bi-monthly by the Chilliwack parish priest at St. Ann's mission, on Old Yale Road, east of Abbotsford, beginning in 1913. When the parish was officially established in 1929, the little church was moved to Gladys and Hazel, and served by a resident priest.

The first Baptist church in the area was organized by Swedish settlers in Matsqui in 1910. In 1973, the congregation moved from the village of Matsqui to Abbotsford.

The Church of the Nazarene began in 1924, while the Pentecostal Tabernacle started in 1926.

After the first German-speaking Mennonites moved into the area in 1928, Mennonite Brethren established the South Abbotsford MB Church in 1932, while the General Conference of Mennonites founded West Abbotsford in 1936.

West Abbotsford Mennonite Church, 1936

The emigration of a number of Russian Orthodox families from Europe in 1926 soon led to the organization of a congregation. Mrs. Faina Pichugin donated the land for a place of worship. The octagonal Russian Orthodox Chapel of St. Peter and St. Paul was dedicated on December 31, 1934. When attendance dwindled, Holy Day services were conducted from Vancouver sporadically. Eventually the icons (sacred pictures) were moved to the Holy Resurrection Church of Vancouver, and the chapel closed in 1972–73.

Russian Orthodox Chapel of St. Peter & St. Paul

The Seventh Day Adventist church began

(l.to r.) Rev. Kizum, Mrs. Kouritzin and Faina Pichugin

in 1943, Grace Church in 1946, and the Christian & Missionary Alliance in 1948.

The Christian Reformed Church was established by Dutch immigrants in 1950, though they had been meeting regularly in various locations in the area since 1929, and many had been members of the church in Sumas beginning in 1937. The First CRC established Gifford Chapel. The Reformed Church conducted its first service in 1954.

The Evangelical Free Church dates its beginning here to 1958, while the Free Methodists started in 1983.

Many additional churches of the various denominational groups were founded over the years. The impact of over sixty Christian churches in the area who belong to the Matsqui–Abbotsford Ministerial Association cannot be underestimated.

Gifford Chapel

The Churches in the Heart of the Valley

1. St. Matthew's Anglican Church

St. Matthew's, one of the first churches in the area, built at the turn of the century on donated land, was dedicated on October 28, 1900. It seated 100. The village of Abbotsford did not exist at the time and Clearbrook was a wilderness. People came many miles on foot, horseback or in wagons. Ten pounds sterling would have paid all the debts. Until 1908, a succession of ministers conducted the services. One of them walked from Mission to Abbotsford and back each Sunday for several years, crossing the Fraser River on the railway bridge.

St. Matthew's Church, 1900

A succession of rectors and many faithful saints gave of their time, money and talents, and have now passed on. The church went through three decades of upheaval: World War I, the Great Depression and World War II. Rev. Norman Calland, one of our most memorable ministers, loved not only by Anglicans but by the community as well, served from 1951 to 1972.

St. Matthew's Church, Montvue Street, 1970

The first significant turning point occurred after Rev. Charles Bryce became rector in 1972. Since the church was bulging at the seams, no further growth or ministry to the community could occur without a larger, more modern facility. In 1974, after many trials and tribulations, property was purchased on Marshall Road, but the corner-stone was not laid until 1977. After the new church was dedicated by Bishop Somerville on October 9, 1977, the expected growth was realized.

When Rev. Bryce retired in 1979, we had a beautiful new facility, thanks largely to his vision and determination.

The next major turning point in St. Matthew's 80-year history came under the kind and loving leadership of the next rector, Rev. Jack Major.

Vicarage beside St. Matthew's on Montvue

Great changes and growth occurred when the "Praise Folk" started to lead the singing at the new 9:15 family Eucharist. Other changes included regular healing services, a food cupboard organized to help people in need, Rev. Jack's discretionary fund providing temporary assistance for the needy, Bible study classes, prayer counsellors, and a quarterly parish magazine.

It took 75 years to outgrow the first church, but only ten to outgrow the new sanctuary. Another upheaval occurred. Under the guidance of Rev. Major, the present sanctuary was built on the Marshall Road premises. At the present time, St. Matthew's Anglican Church functions under the new leadership of the Rev. Dr. Trevor Walters and assistant, Rev. Bill Inglis.

The "Parish Purpose" is, "with God's help, to develop a loving fellow-ship in Christ, through which the gifts and talents of each person are offered to the glory of God." Today, the Gospel of love and reconciliation is being preached. The unchurched are finding a church home and a lov-ing welcome. Lives are being changed. People are being healed physically and spiritually. While retaining our tradi-tional Anglican roots, we are also evangeli-cal and charismatic, so that all may find a form of worship they are comfortable with. St. Matthew's con-tinues to grow and already, after only five years, some ser-vices are filled to capacity. Our hope

Archbishop David Somerville laying the cornerstone for the new facility, April 1977.

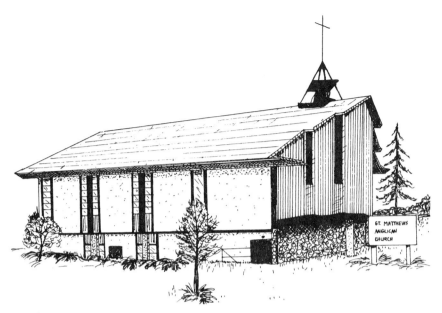

1980 Sanctuary

and vision is to work toward starting a daughter congregation in the western part of the community. With God's help, we will go forward in faith.

Facilities of the Parish Church of Saint Matthew

2. Abbotsford Baptist Church

Knowing what has happened in the past helps us know who we are now, so we can face the future with confidence. This is also true for the church.

Eighty-two years ago, on March 16, 1910, the First Baptist Church of Matsqui, now known as Abbotsford Baptist Church, was organized. Eighteen Swedish immigrants from the Champion Street Baptist Church in Bellingham, along with their pastor, Rev. Charles Asplund and 18 local people organized the church. Rev. P. A. Peterson, the first pastor, divided his time between Vancouver and Matsqui.

Two things were very real to the early pioneers who met for Bible reading and prayer in their little homes: the living presence of Jesus Christ as their Saviour and Lord, and a fresh word from that Lord in His Book, the Bible. Those were the two most precious parts of our heritage that they bequeathed to us. They are the strengths of our past: the Lordship of Jesus Christ and the authority of the Bible.

Stanley Carlson, who came to Matsqui with his parents in 1910, recalls how he and his parents, charter members, walked six miles to the school where the first services were held, before the building was completed in Matsqui village. The church was plagued by problems during many of its 60 years, including the fact that the Swedish language isolated them from their neighbours.

The little congregation in Matsqui experienced God's special leading during two disasters. In 1934 their church building burned to the ground.

Original First Baptist Church, Matsqui

Congregation, 1910

But out of the ashes rose a new, nicer building. In spring, 1948, the Fraser River flood inundated the whole Matsqui prairie. During that disaster, people rowed out to the church in a boat, looked in through the windows and saw the yellow pine pews floating inside, the tops of their backs near the ceiling. Yet, after the flood, when the silt had been removed, the church was restored to its former condition and use: a Gospel light that the flood could not put out.

Outstanding service was rendered to the church and community by Edward S. Eklund, who died in February, 1967, after having served for 40 years as Sunday School superintendent as well as vice-chairman and clerk of the church. Other supportive people in the congregation included the Stan Carlsons, the Helmer Kvists, Sheila Trotter and the Grant Riddles. Dr. Herbert H. Janson, a professor at Vancouver Bible College, was led by God to begin pastoral ministry at First Baptist Church. Through his determined ministry, the church began to grow. He preached, visited and encouraged the handful of people he found there and the Lord fanned the flickering torch into a glowing witness.

When Rev. William Funk began his Matsqui pastorate, August 1, 1971. Two years later, it purchased a vacant church edifice on Busby Street in Abbotsford from the Grace Church. The congregation moved

Matsqui Baptist Church

15

Abbotsford Baptist Church

five miles south, into town, and took the new name: Abbotsford Baptist Church.

Douglas and Helen Johnson had come to Abbotsford in 1974 and served as associate pastor for seven and a half years. He was ordained by the church on November 27, 1976. Rev. Johnson's official pastorate ended in October, 1981. Nevertheless, he continues to serve in the music ministry. Mr. Brian Rapske came for a five-year pastorate in February, 1980. His pastorate climaxed with the church's 75th anniversary in 1985. He left the church to seek further education.

Rev. Roger McClelland, his wife Vicki and son Lyle, came from Bethel Theological Seminary West in San Diego, California, to pastor the Abbotsford Baptist Church, commencing January 1, 1986.

The strength of our heritage as a church is the living presence of Jesus Christ and a fresh word from Him in the Bible. "Jesus in the heart, the Bible in the hand." So simple, so naive, so strong!

If Christ is everything and His Word is our guide, then His presence can illumine our church meetings and make them times when heaven comes down to earth and we experience what those 18 Swedish immigrants experienced in their little houses, scattered across the farmlands of Matsqui some 82 years ago: Jesus in our hearts, the Bible in our hands.

3. Immanuel Baptist Church

The pastor and people of Aldergrove Fellowship Baptist Church had a desire to plant a daughter church. So Rev. Sam McCallum and eleven people who worshipped at Aldergrove but lived in Clearbrook, prayed for guidance in founding a new work here.

A year later they saw a definite answer to their prayers. A young man who had graduated from the Grand Rapids Baptist Seminary came for a week of orientation, and Jack and Jane Glupker met with the interested people. In November 1984, Pastor Jack received a unanimous call to take over the new work in the Clearbrook–Abbotsford area. The Lion's Loft in the Abbotsford Community Centre was rented by this new Home Mission Church and forty-three people attended the inaugural service. An electric keyboard was used to accompany the singing. When the average attendance reached thirty-five, it became necessary to find larger quarters.

In the summer of 1985 the church moved to the auditorium of Chief Dan George Elementary School. Members of the church visited residents of the area to let them know about the new church. Prior to the first service at Chief Dan George School, a celebration concert was held to praise the Lord for His goodness. Al Willms was the soloist.

By mid-September, Sunday School classes were formed and a sound system purchased. One hundred new chairs and hymnbooks from the Kamloops Baptist Church were in use. During the week, a trailer housed the equipment. Because of numerical growth, additional chairs had to be purchased,

Rev. Jack and Mrs. Jane Glupker, founding pastor of Immanuel Baptist Church.

and in September 1991, a closed truck was acquired to store all the equipment.

A Christian Service Brigade was formed as an outreach for boys. At Thanksgiving time, food hampers were distributed to needy families. Weekly prayer meetings and Bible study, combined with excellent teaching on Sunday, provided solid spiritual food for those in attendance. Participation in a missions conference with friends at the Aldergrove Baptist Church was a highlight.

The first baptismal service was held on March 19, 1984, followed by others in succeeding years. Special music provided by those in our church and talented guests, enhanced our times of worship.

Blue Jay Elementary School, meetingplace of Immanuel Baptist Church.

In 1987 we were able to purchase a lot in the Blue Jay area for a future church building. At an ordination service held in our mother church in Aldergrove, Pastor Glupker become the Rev. Glupker. This was a happy occasion.

A Family Week was held at Camp Quanoes on Vancouver Island, with Pastor Glupker teaching the Word. Family Camp has now become a regular event.

In 1988 associate pastor Brennan Basler and family came to minister to our youth. Adventure Day Camp, held each summer, has been a means of reaching children in the neighbourhood.

Volunteers remodelled a trailer for use as an office, which was placed on the new church property on Old Yale Road. Population in this area grew beyond all expectations and the new Blue Jay Elementary School became the logical place to hold future Sunday services. We began meeting there before school began in 1988.

Two of our young men have studied the Bible at Capernwray, one in Austria and one in Australia. Their sister has been accepted as a missionary and hopes to leave for service in France in 1992.

Since the Northwest Baptist Theological Bible College and Seminary has moved to the campus of Trinity Western University, several faculty and staff members have located in our area. They and their families have joined our church and have been a blessing.

After seven years of helpful ministry, Pastor Glupker tendered his resignation, concluding his service on the last Sunday in January. Our love and prayers go with them as they seek the Lord's place for further service.

All of us at Immanuel Fellowship Baptist Church continue to look to God for blessing as we serve Him in this part of His vineyard. We want to see lost souls saved and Christians built up in their faith.

4. Maranatha Baptist Church

Maranatha Baptist Church on Gladys Ave.

Maranatha Baptist Church had its beginnings in the fall of 1973, when a group of six believers began meeting on a weekly basis in a private home in the Abbotsford area.

January 1974 brought a move to rented facilities on Gladys Avenue, Abbotsford, where attendance increased. Pastor John Crook and his wife Eleanore, both retired missionaries who had been expelled from Communist China, led this fledgling group. In 1975 the group organized

Pastor & Mrs. John Crook

Pastor Wesley DeZeeuw

Maranatha Baptist Church, Old Yale Road

Pastor Joseph & Sylvia Ratcliffe

Pastor & Mrs. Mackay

into a local Baptist Church, affiliated with the Baptist Union of Western Canada, and in February 1976 the name Maranatha Baptist Church was chosen.

In 1976 property was purchased at 33393 Old Yale Road and on November 6, 1976 student pastor Wesley DeZeeuw held the first service in the new premises. The congregation grew until it became evident in 1985 that larger facilities were required.

Maranatha Baptist purchased on Clearbrook Road, adjacent to Clearbrook Elementary School and an ambitious building program began. During the interim between the sale of the Old Yale Road prop-

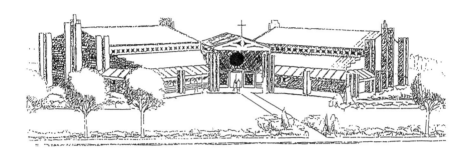

Architect's drawing of present facilities

erty and the completion of the new building, services were conducted at Columbia Bible Institute. The present church was completed November 1988 and the service of dedication held in December with Rev. Joseph Ratcliffe as pastor. In December 1990 Rev. Ed Mackay from Victoria arrived to assume leadership of the congregation.

Church activities include Junior Adventure Hour, youth groups, young adult and young families groups, home Bible studies, ladies Bible studies, Golden Agers, and a special outreach into the community through an English as a Second Language program.

Sunday services begin at 9:50 AM with Sunday school for all ages immediately following the worship service. Evening services begin at 6:30 PM. Further information can be obtained by calling 854-1505 Monday through Friday AM.

A warm and friendly welcome awaits everyone at our location, 3580 Clearbrook Road.

"Come as a visitor — Leave as a friend."

5. Saint Ann's Parish

Saint Ann's was officially established as a parish of the Archdiocese of Vancouver in 1929 by decision of Archbishop William Mark Duke. It serves Catholics within a territory bounded on the north by Harris Road on the Matsqui prairie, on the east by the Vedder Canal, on the south by the international boundary, and on the west by Mt. Lehman Road. There are currently about 1500 families in the parish.

Before 1929, Catholics in this area were served by visiting priests, chiefly Oblate fathers from Mission City. From 1910, Sunday Mass was celebrated in the home of the de la Giroday family, where a large room was reserved as a chapel. (This pioneer residence is still standing, occupied by other members of the parish.)

In 1913, Catholics were able to move to their own church located on the crest of the Old Yale Road, east of the railway station. During the following years, two fires caused extensive damage to the church and hardship for the small community.

With the founding of the parish in 1929, the old church building was moved down the hill to a site on the Mission highway. A small rectory was built next door and the church was enlarged in 1935 and again in 1949.

Saint Ann's, 1929–1966

Saint Ann's Catholic Church, 33333 Mayfair

By the mid sixties, the need for a new building to accommodate the growing parish family was met with the move to a new nine-acre site, now bisected by Mayfair Avenue. A church with seating for almost 500 was blessed in 1966. The bell from the old church was relocated to a new tower and still calls parishioners to worship every Sunday morning.

In the ensuing years, the parish grew at the same rapid rate as the community at large. In the near future, we expect a new parish to be established in Clearbrook, to serve the Catholic community in that part of the district.

A highlight for Catholics across Canada was the 1984 visit of Pope John Paul II. Saint Ann's was involved in a special way, as the Pope celebrated Mass with over 250,000 people within the parish boundaries, at the Abbotsford airport.

Over the years, the children of the parish received catechism lessons from dedicated volunteers, for several years using rented classrooms in Abbotsford Junior High School, adjacent to the church.

In 1985, a new era in Catholic education began with the opening of Saint Ann's elementary school on a seventeen-acre site off Old Yale Road in Clearbrook. Since its opening the school population has grown to 185 pupils taught by a lay staff of twelve. When at full capacity, the school will enroll over 200 students from kindergarten to grade seven. At the same time, over 300 Catholic children who attend public schools receive weekly religious instruction on weekday evenings using the school facilities. Over 30 parishioners serve as volunteer catechists in this program.

The centennial year of Matsqui will mark another landmark in Catholic education: the opening of the first grades of a new regional Catholic high school, developed by Saint Ann's and neighbouring parishes, to serve students from Chilliwack, Abbotsford, Matsqui, Aldergrove, Langley and Mission. This new school will be located on its own ten-acre site, adjacent to Saint Ann's elementary school. In September of 1992, the first grade eight classes will begin in portable classrooms and the construction of a permanent facility will commence at the same time. When fully grown, the new school will enroll upwards of 700 students.

Saint Ann's Catholic School

Of course, statistics tell only part of the story. Less tangible but more important is the story of faith and commitment that inspires people to work together to build a parish community and to serve the wider community in many different ways. In this spiritual dimension of faith, hope and charity, the real history of a parish is known. The heritage we celebrate in this centennial year is the lives and example of people of faith: laymen and women and priests who went before us and planted the seed of the Church which is flourishing today.

6. Sevenoaks Alliance Church

THE CHRISTIAN & MISSIONARY ALLIANCE

What is the Christian and Missionary Alliance? It is a Protestant denomination focused on world missions. More than a century ago, Alliance founder Dr. A.B. Simpson left a New York Presbyterian pulpit to reach out to neglected people around the world.

Today the Alliance has a world-wide constituency of over two million members in over 10,000 churches. Our missions and national church leaders are working in 54 countries telling millions about the love of Jesus Christ. The well known Christian and Missionary Alliance logo of the cross, pitcher, cup and crown signify Christ as our Saviour, Sanctifier, Healer and Coming King.

BEGINNINGS

Significant events in the early months of 1948 led to the formation of Abbotsford Alliance Church, now known as Sevenoaks Alliance. In the late 40's, Chilliwack Alliance was sponsoring a radio program covering the Valley. Rev. Alf Orthner conducted several Sunday afternoon "Radio Rallies" in the Phillip Sheffield High School auditorium. Crowds of up to 700 attended these rallies. Soon several Abbotsford families began

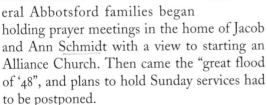
Abbotsford Alliance first met in the Eagles' Hall

holding prayer meetings in the home of Jacob and Ann Schmidt with a view to starting an Alliance Church. Then came the "great flood of '48", and plans to hold Sunday services had to be postponed.

Providentially, just when conditions were beginning to improve, a young Bible School student from the Alliance school in Regina was available for ministry. John Thomson travelled from Vancouver to Abbotsford twice weekly throughout the summer to conduct

Clem Dreger 1948–1952

Alliance Tabernacle, 1956

prayer fellowship meetings as well as Sunday services in the Schmidt home. By mid-August the Sunday services were moved to the old Eagles' Hall with 60 present at the first service there. After the Thomsons returned to Bible School in Regina, the church welcomed its first fulltime resident pastor, Rev. Clement Dreger on Sept. 24, 1948.

SENIOR PASTORS AND HIGHLIGHTS

The congregation began its first building project on Alliance Street and began using the basement auditorium in 1950.

The sanctuary was completed a few years later and a gym was added in 1963.

Pastors during those years included George Magnus 1952–53, Eric Berg 1953–56, Norman Dreger 1956–62, Grant Hastie 1962–64, and Milton Johnson 1964–72.

During 1970, a significant revival under the leadership of the Sutera Twins of Ohio resulted in much growth.

With steady growth, a huge step of faith was taken: the purchase of choice property at 2575 Gladwin Road and erection of new facilities in June, 1971.

A team concept of pastoral ministry grew in May, 1973. A surge of growth increased attendance to over 2000. During this period

William Goetz 1973–90

Alliance Church, 1971

Dedication of Sevenoaks Alliance Sanctuary Sept. 23, 1983

Albert Runge 1991–

the name was changed from Abbotsford Alliance to Sevenoaks Alliance Church. With varying degrees of help from Sevenoaks, churches were planted in Mission, Langley, Aldergrove and Clearbrook. At the same time, Sevenoaks Alliance constructed a new sanctuary.

A much-appreciated relationship with both neighboring malls developed whereby they shared their parking lot with us on Sunday and had access to ours on weekdays.

Henry Wiebe served as interim senior pastor during 1990–91.

After a year's prayerful search, Sevenoaks Alliance welcomed a new senior pastor, Al Runge, on Easter Sunday, March 31, 1991.

EMPHASES

At least eight priorities served to foster the growth and impact of Sevenoaks Alliance Church during the Goetz era.

1. Prayer is fostered individually and in groups.
2. Love for God, His Word, His people and the spiritually lost motivate the believers to action.
3. Spiritual gifts are used by each Christian as the Holy Spirit directs.
4. Evangelism provides for effective, ongoing outreach.
5. Preaching — a strong pulpit voice is provided by enlisting the gifts of a preaching pastor.
6. Missions — "missionary" is the middle name of the Alliance. The annual World Missions Week is the highlight of the year. Giving to missions reached $624,630 in 1991. Over 50 people in full-time Christian service at home or abroad consider Sevenoaks Alliance as

Jack Campbell, Africa

Julie Fehr, Gabon

Harold Priebe, Venezuela

Kathy (Neetz) Cobb, Guinea

Missionary Residence

Avril (Klassen) Crundwell, Venezuela

their home church. Among them are five pictured here.

A furnished missionary home has been made available to missionaries on furlough. The missionary's rental allowance carries the mortgage.

7. Programs provide effective ministries to all age groups.

8. Publicity through advertising, posters, promotions, etc., ensures that the word is out.

The purpose statement, coat-of-aims and logo summarizes the vision and gives the people a unified thrust. Pastoral leadership is supported by shepherding elders, the board of elders and the ministering staff.

"The purpose of the Sevenoaks Alliance Church is to produce worshipping, caring, Spirit-filled mature disciples who fulfill the Great Commission by winning people to Christ and leading them in becoming reproducing members of this Global Impact Family."

A NEW ERA

When Albert and Lee Runge arrived he stated, "Our view of ministry is to care for the spiritual and social needs of people. We trusting the Lord for a great future as we seek together to glorify God and help people."

Children's choir

Sevenoaks Alliance Complex

7. HERITAGE ALLIANCE CHURCH

The seed of Heritage Alliance was planted in February of 1988. After a committee was formed through the elders board of Sevenoaks Alliance Church, several couples began meeting to pray for God's direction. As God brought more people together, social events were planned along with the prayer meetings. In December 1988 over one hundred people gathered for a Christmas celebration dinner. The new church was beginning to sprout!

Rev. Jack & Gladys Schroeder

A pastor seasoned in church planting, Rev. Jack and Gladys Schroeder accepted the call. What an exciting day, when on February 19, 1989 the doors of MEI were opened and Heritage Alliance celebrated the first service with an attendance of 306! On May 28, 1989, charter Sunday, 100 charter members joined. Over the past 3 years, steady growth has taken place. The hallmark of Heritage is an emphasis on the family: people of all ages fellowshipping together and caring for one another as they grow together in their faith in Christ. The unique needs of our growing children's and youth ministry are looked after by staff members, C.E. director Jan Heppner, and youth pastor Don Dewey.

CONCLUSION

The Christian & Missionary Alliance in Canada will convene its General Assembly in the Matsqui–Abbotsford area during this centennial year of 1992. June 20 to 28 will see such events as a Conference on the Family, a Conference for Missionaries, public meetings, business sessions, and luncheons culminating in a banquet at Tradex where tribute will be paid to outgoing president Dr. Melvin Sylvester. Three missionary rallies on Sunday afternoon and evening will close the Assembly. As a church we thank this community for its cooperation and look forward to serving you in the future.

Introduction to the Christian Reformed Denomination

The Christian Reformed Churches in our area belong to a denomination that has been in existence since the mid 1800's. Dutch men and women, tired of poverty and persecution in the Netherlands, fled to North America. These Dutch immigrants, followers of John Calvin, established and maintained their own congregations. These small congregations grew into a denomination — the Christian Reformed Church.

Reformed Christians share with others the belief that the Bible is God's Word. We view it as the historical record of God's saving deeds by which He calls persons to new life and to obedience. We believe that we are saved by grace. Therefore, we also believe in election and practice infant baptism, a doctrine and a sacrament which clearly declare that God's grace is first.

Each Christian Reformed church worships a little differently. The sermon is the most prominent part of our worship service.

Reformed Christians serve the Lord in this life, believing it is a part of eternal life. We view the Christian life not as a Sunday-only matter, but as a seven day a week commitment. That commitment demands participation in missions, evangelism, education, labour and politics.

To be Reformed means to live what we believe. We share with most Christian churches the three ecumenical creeds: the Apostles Creed, the Nicene Creed, and the Athanasian Creed. We accept three Reformed confessions: the Heidelberg Catechism, the Belgic Confession and the Canons of Dort.

One word that expresses what is unique about the Reformed understanding of the Christian faith is the word SOVEREIGN. We believe that God is Sovereign. He is King. Because He is creator of all that exists, His laws and norms hold for the whole creation. The world belongs to Him.

It is a challenge to be a Reformed Christian. It is exciting to be part of, to share joys and sorrows with, to rest and to work with the group of Christians known as the Christian Reformed Church, not because they are quaint or special, but because the sovereign Creator's grace is at work among us.

CHRISTIAN REFORMED CHURCHES
IN THE ABBOTSFORD–MATSQUI AREA

By the year 1929 a small group of settlers of Christian Reformed background had settled in the Glen Valley, among them the Jansen family (see photo).

These people were either newly arrived immigrants from the Netherlands or older settlers from other parts of Canada.

At first the group met for worship every Sunday afternoon in a house at 264th and River Road, but during 1930 and 1931 they used the facilities of the East Langley School. Then services were held in the Jansen home till early 1937. The service was always conducted in the Dutch language. Often, one of the men would read a sermon, but once per month the service was conducted by an ordained minister, usually by the well-known Rev. Peter Hoekstra.

By 1937 most of these people had left Glen Valley. Several of them joined the Sumas, Washington, Christian Reformed Church. During the late thirties and the Second World War other families from Alberta and other parts of B.C. joined them.

In this the centennial year of the District of Matsqui there are five Christian Reformed Churches in our area. They are the First Christian Reformed Church at 1951 McCallum Road, the Second Christian Reformed Church at 34631 Old Clayburn road, Trinity Christian Reformed Church at 3215 Trethewey Street in Clearbrook, Zion Christian Reformed Church at 35199 Delair Road, and New Life Christian Reformed Church presently worshipping in the Abbotsford Christian Secondary School on Old Clayburn Road.

Following the Second World War numerous immigrants from the Netherlands flocked into Canada. Many of them were dairy farmers and

Meeting at Jansen home

settled in British Columbia and especially in the Fraser Valley where the land was fertile and the future promising.

Most of these people were deeply religious and not only concerned with the material but also with the spiritual well-being of their families. For them, being part of a church community was as important as establishing themselves financially in their adopted country. Most of them had belonged to the Calvinistic Reformed Sister Churches of the Christian Reformed Denomination, but since there was no Christian Reformed Church in the area at the time, they joined the "Old Timers" in travelling to the Sumas Christian Reformed Church. Customs officers usually let them pass with a wave of the hand, knowing they would all return within a couple of hours.

The Sumas congregation, a well-established church, conducted all services in English. The newly arrived immigrants spoke and understood minimal English. But they treasured the singing and the communion of the believers. From these services they derived the renewal of spirit and strength to face another week of hard work. They never complained!

When more and more immigrants arrived, a meeting was conducted by Rev. Paul De Koekkoek on November 15, 1949, at which it was decided to form a church in Abbotsford. At first this group met in the Back to God Chapel on Vye Road across from the Upper Sumas School. Then, while a committee searched for suitable property, they worshipped in the Hungarian Presbyterian Church in Abbotsford. Soon the search committee proposed buying a 13-acre property with an old garage on it on the Abbotsford–Mission Highway for $5,125.00. The building was converted, transforming the old garage into a church!

On the evening of October 13, 1950 the First Christian Reformed Church was organized. Rev. W. VerWolf and elders Advocaat and Likkel of the Sumas Church were in charge of the organizational meeting.

Rev. VerWolf spoke on Isaiah 54:2 and 3: "Enlarge the place of thy tent and let them stretch forth the curtains of thine habitations, spare not, lengthen thy cords and strengthen thy stakes for thou shalt break forth on the right and on the left." The words turned out to be prophetic.

A total of one hundred forty people (men, women, and children) became members at that time. The first consistory consisted of elders Peter Kooy, Cornelius Ingwersen, Tinus DeJong, Douwe DeVries and deacons Andy Nanninga and Jake Hoogendoorn. Services were held every Sunday at 10:30 AM and 2:00 PM. One was conducted in Dutch, the other in English.

In July 1951 the Rev. DeKoekkoek left and Rev. Betten took over until Rev. John Roorda arrived in 1953.

The influx of immigrants continued unabated and the church building became too small. In 1954 the property on Mission Highway was transferred to the Christian School Society and used until 1989, when the original building was demolished (see photos). The congregation bought 1½ acres of land at the corner of McCallum and Holland Roads for $2,000.00 and built the present First Christian Reformed Church of Abbotsford. The dedication service was held February 23, 1955.

Early in 1957 Rev. Roorda left for Escondido, California, but even though the church had no pastor till well into 1958, it continued to grow. The Rev. Titus Heyboer took up pastoral duties on January 9, 1959 and served until May, 1969.

During the 1960's a high birth rate, continuous immigration, and families arriving from other parts of Canada, kept the church growing.

In 1962 outreach into the community was begun when the Gifford Sunday School was started and the Back to God Hour premiered on CFVR. Both ventures have been carried on till the present.

In 1966, when three services were conducted at First Church each Sunday, a committee was struck to plan for a Second Christian Reformed Church in our

First Christian Reformed Church, Mission Highway

community. In 1967 a four-acre site was purchased on Old Clayburn Road and planning for a second congregation started in earnest.

The organization of the Second Christian Reformed Church took place on March 3, 1969, and since the congregation had no church building, worship services were held in the same premises where the First Church had started: the old building on Mission Highway!

The first pastor, Rev. Marvin Heyboer, preached his inaugural sermon on August 31, 1969 and the new church building on Old Clayburn Road was dedicated February 19, 1970.

As the growth in both churches continued, plans were made for starting a third church in the Abbotsford–Matsqui area. During the summer of 1977 sign-up lists were placed in First and Second Church for interested families. When enough signatures had been gathered, the first meeting of the new church took place on August 28, 1977 in the MEI auditorium at the corner of Clearbrook and Old Yale Roads. The official organization of the church took place in the evening of October 31, 1977.

Almost immediately plans were made to build a new church at the corner of Maclure and Trethewey. The dedication service of the church was held on December 19, 1978. The first pastor, Rev. Dick Stienstra, was installed on September 7, 1978. He served the congregation till the end of 1984, when he accepted a call to the Dundas Christian Reformed Church. From 1986 till 1991 Rev. Henry Numan was the pastor at Trinity.

The Zion Christian Reformed Church was started as a ministry to refugees from Indo–China. Its first service was held on November 4, 1979 at Trinity Christian Reformed Church. The Rev. Stephen Jung preached in Cantonese every Sunday until Rev. Livingstone Chen took over full-time pastoral care of the congregation in September 1981.

During the years that followed, more and more people from the local Chinese community became involved with Zion church and became active members, serving with their time and talents.

From September 1982 till 1991 the congregation shared the facilities of the First Christian Reformed Church. Since then they worship in their own new church on Delair Road.

On April 15, 1986 a meeting was held in the gymnasium of the Christian Elementary School on Mission Highway to discuss the feasibility of starting yet another Christian Reformed Church. Elders from First and Second Christian Reformed Churches explained that both of their churches were overcrowded during Sunday morning services and therefore the organization of another church seemed feasible.

It soon became evident that this new church would be different from the other older established ones. Influenced by the charismatic movement sweeping North America, many of the people present expressed the desire for more participation and freedom of expression in worship services. An agreement was reached that this would be the future direction of the new church. The name New Life Christian Reformed Church was chosen indicating the new life we share with all who believe in the Lord Jesus Christ as their Saviour and Lord.

The organizational meeting took place on November 20, 1986. The congregation presently uses the facilities of the Abbotsford Christian Secondary School for worship services and programs. However, property has been bought on Delair Road and plans are being made to build a church there in the near future. Rev. John Poortenga has pastored this congregation since January 1988.

8. The First Christian Reformed Church of Abbotsford

> We are
> people committed to living to the glory of God
> and providing as a church
> worship, education
> fellowship and member care
> witness and service
> so that many people become disciples of Jesus Christ,
> serving him with life-style obedience in this world.

After Rev. Titus Heyboer, pastor Peter VanEgmond served the congregation form 1969 to 1980. He witnessed the formation of Second Christian Reformed Church and Trinity Christian Reformed Church,

Original First Christian Reformed Church, McCallum Road

both daughter churches of the First Church. He also saw the erection of the Ebenezer Home on Marshall Road. This home was erected with the help of the deacons of the B.C. churches and still receives support from the Christian Reformed Churches. Although the First Church is in charge, the various Christian Reformed Churches carry out a vital ministry in this home. When pastor VanEgmond left for Toronto, Ontario, in 1980, he was followed by pastor Alvin Beukema.

First Church remained a large congregation of more than 185 families, some 700 to 800 members, young and old. Help was needed. First Bob and Ineke Lodewyk came. Bob was a graduate of the Reformed Bible Institute in Grand Rapids, Michigan, U.S.A. He was deeply involved in the work of evangelism and took care of the Gifford Chapel. He served First Church for three years. Now Bob and Ineke serve the Lord in Nigeria.

Even though the formation of New Life Christian Reformed Church took some 35 young families out of First Church, the work still could not be done by one pastor. For three years in a row seminarians were engaged. As part of their training at Calvin Seminary in Grand Rapids, each seminarian had to serve one year in a congregation. First Church was well-served by the following seminary students. Henry Steenbergen

(1987–1988) concentrated on the young families. After graduation from Calvin Seminary, he became a regular pastor in Brighton, Ontario. Peter Vellenga (1988–1989) carried out his training as student pastor by caring for the Young Adults. While with us he was single, but now he is married and has graduated from Calvin Seminary. Presently he is pastor of the Independent Christian Reformed Church in Aylmer, Ontario. Bruce Adema (1989–1990), the last seminarian, faced unexpected challenges due to the sudden and frequent eye surgeries of his supervisor pastor. In the summer of 1992 he hopes to be declared candidate for the ministry in the Christian Reformed Church.

Although each seminarian contributed to the congregation with his gifts, their presence was temporary. A more permanent solution was found when pastor Bert Slofstra came in September 1990. The congregation now enjoys the services of a team of two pastors. A staff ministry is developing since First Church has already appointed a part-time music director, Mrs. Betty Lieuwen, and has adopted the recommendation to call a Youth Pastor. Mrs. Betty-Lou VanKampen, a daughter of one of the former ministers, serves as part-time secretary.

In 1982 a fellowship hall and kitchen, a large nursery, a secretarial office and pastor's study as well as a fine Church Council facility were built. The entrance to the church building improved drastically. First Church also acquired the adjacent property with a small house on it at 33569 Rainbow from Mr. Bill VanderSpek, Jr. and recently adopted the recommendation to buy the corner lot with house at Rainbow and McCallum. First Church has gone on record to rebuild, but the location has yet to be determined.

The Church continues to follow the Reformed faith, is known to be conservative and ever seeks to be a blessing for her members and the community. With great commitment and dedication, First Church supports many denominational outreaches and contributes liberally to the Christian Reformed World Relief Committee. Needy persons receive help from the deacons. Every year Daily Vacation Bible Schools are held both in First Church and in Gifford Chapel.

First Christian Reformed Church, 1951 McCallum Road today

9. THE SECOND CHRISTIAN REFORMED CHURCH OF ABBOTSFORD

When the First Christian Reformed Church had outgrown its facilities, 58 families and seven single members were willing to form the new congregation.

The organizational meeting took place on March 3, 1969 in First Church, presided over by Rev. T. Heyboer, who opened the evening with a sermon on Psalm 127:1a "Unless the Lord builds the house, they that build it labour in vain."

Thanks to the foresight of First Church's consistory, the mother church had already purchased a property in an area where no churches existed. A generous gift of $10,000.00 and the property on Old Clayburn Road were two ways by which First Church helped her new daughter.

The new congregation found a temporary place of worship in the old school gym on the Mission Highway. Rev. John Hoffman from Lynden conducted the first service on March 23, 1969.

After Rev. Gerald Vandenberg declined the call to pastor the new congregation, candidate Marvin Heyboer of Grand Rapids, accepted. A parsonage belonging to the Canadian Reformed Church was rented till July 15, 1970.

The Building Committee obtained a set of plans for a new church,

Second Christian Reformed Church, 34631 Old Clayburn Road

designed by Mr. Dewey De Vries Jr. from Surrey. When the late Mike Lindeboom explained the plans, the congregation approved the construction in two stages: a) the fellowship hall and educational wing, b) the sanctuary.

By the middle of February 1970 the new congregation occupied its own place of worship. A parsonage was completed during the summer of 1970. When the congregation grew rapidly from 58 to 140 families it became clear that the sanctuary was badly needed.

The congregation approved the plan on April 17, 1972. Although Mr. Lindeboom would have loved to complete the building program, the Lord called him home on October 22, 1972. Sid Bos supervised the construction of the sanctuary. In the meantime, a used pipe organ from the Masonic Temple had been purchased for $3500.00 and installed by Bert Blok Sr. and Bert Blok Jr. The new sanctuary was dedicated on Sunday, February 11, 1973 during the morning service. In the evening worship service Pastor Heyboer preached his farewell sermon.

Under the leadership of pastors Marvin Heyboer (1969–1973), Harry Mennega (1973–1979) and Aubrey VanHoff (1980–1989) our church was blessed with the preaching of Christ-centered sermons and weekly activities. A typical calendar of such activities reads:

Monday: Children's Choir practice
                    Calvinettes and Cadets clubs for ages 9–14

Tuesday: Ladies Bible Study Group meets in the morning.
                    In the evening students from grades 8–12 receive instruction in God's Word, reflected in the three Reformed Confessions.
                    A class for all ages meets with the pastor for Bible study.

Wednesday: Coffee Break & Story Hour Evangelism during the morning hours, an outreach program in the community, an informal time of Bible Study and fellowship for mothers and children. A nursery looks after the babies and toddlers.

Thursday: Choir practice

Friday: Shopping night

Saturday: Breakfast meeting of a group of men, called Men's Life, discussing the Word of God.

Sunday: Worship services at 10:00 AM and 7:00 PM.
                    After the evening service the youth meets in core groups and Teen Club. Various districts also meet in growth groups, focusing on Bible Study.

Outreach takes an important place, morally and/or financially in support of such organizations as:
    The Christian Reformed World Relief Committee

Back to God Hour Radio Broadcast and TV hour
Ebenezer Senior Home
Bethesda Christian Association for the Handicapped
Home Missions, Harbour Missions, World Missions
Telecare and Food Bank

During the summer months a Vacation Bible School is conducted for the neighbourhood children, where the old, old story of Jesus and His love is told.

In 1990 two new pastors, namely Rev. C. Harry Salomons and Youth Pastor Herb de Ruyter, arrived. Both men have accepted the challenge of leading the congregation, dispensing spiritual blessings in the church.

As to the future, we say with the word of Psalm 125: "As the mountains surround Jerusalem, so the Lord surrounds His people both now and forevermore."

In this centennial year let us continue to be a gathering of people who confess Jesus as their Lord.

10. TRINITY CHRISTIAN REFORMED CHURCH OF ABBOTSFORD

Trinity Christian Reformed Church began on October 31, 1977. Due to tremendous growth in the First and Second Christian Reformed Churches of Abbotsford, the councils of these two churches decided to expand the CRC presence in our community by starting a third congregation. Trinity CRC began with approximately 270 members. The first year we worshipped in the basement of the old MEI building at the corner of Old Yale and Clearbrook Roads. Early in 1978 the property on the corner of Maclure and Trethewey was purchased. On August 19, 1978 the newly formed building committee presented church council with a proposal to build phase 1 of a 3-phase building program. Construction began in September. On December 19 and 21, 1978 phase 1 was dedicated by hosting a Community Open House. The congregation continued to grow and in June, 1986, construction of the church sanctuary commenced. On October 29, 1987 the new sanctuary was dedicated, coinciding with the 10th anniversary of Trinity CRC. At this time Trinity has grown to 547 members. In 1990, continued growth necessitated the construction of phase 3: additional classrooms and seating in the balcony of

Trinity Christian Reformed Church, 3215 Trethewey

Interior of Trinity Christian Reformed Church

the sanctuary. In 1987 Trinity adopted a statement of ministry to define its place in the community. It states: "As we have received the Good News, we seek to invite our community to joyful worship, nurture and care in order that all be made whole and equipped to serve."

Throughout the history of this area, churches have played an important role in the spiritual and social development of our community. During the past 100 years, many residents have contributed to the development of the churches in this area. Along with this commitment came many sacrifices. The quality of our community depends greatly now, as it did then, on the freedom to worship and socialize with people of similar convictions. In this framework, God will continue to guide this community and its churches.

ii. ZION CHINESE CHRISTIAN REFORMED CHURCH

The congregation started as a ministry to refugees from Indo–China. Its first service was held at 4 p.m. on November 4, 1979 at Trinity CRC. Thirty people, refugees and their sponsors from local CRC churches attended. Rev. Stephen Jung preached the first sermon in Cantonese. The services continued weekly and refugees from other denominations, such as the Christian and Missionary Alliance and the Mennonite Brethren also started to attend. Rev. Jung carried on this ministry for about two years. Twenty-seven adults were baptized and became the nucleus of this congregation.

Rev. Livingstone Chen arrived in Abbotsford in September 1981. In

亞寶斯福基督教錫安堂

ZION CHINESE CHRISTIAN REFORMED CHURCH

35199 DeLair Road, Box 578, ABBOTSFORD, B.C. V2S 6R7

牧師：林壽華牧師 REV. PAUL LAM

住宅電話：(604) 850-9683

教會電話：(604) 852-9354

October, the name "Zion" was adopted. Although a Co-worker Committee was appointed from within the congregation, volunteers from other churches continued to teach Sunday School and help in the worship service. Attendance hovered around 40 and was unstable.

The congregation moved to the First Christian Reformed Church on September 5, 1982. The members took over more responsibilities from the volunteers. They paid First Church a token rent in addition to taking care of their own program expenses. In January 1983, the attendance grew steadily, partly because a number of Christian families had moved into town. The newcomers readily involved themselves in various ministries and their contagious enthusiasm brought inspiration to the church.

An election was held for the first time on June 10, 1984. The elected Co-worker Committee assisted the pastor in church affairs. By the end of 1984, besides Sunday worship and Sunday school, the ministries included the teens' group, ladies fellowship, adult and junior choirs, a monthly gathering for the elderly and a Chinese school.

The congregation was formally organized as the Zion Christian Reformed Church on May 25, 1986. A few months later, on August 25,

Zion Chinese Christian Reformed Church, 35199 DeLair Road

the church bought a lot of 1.2 acres at 35199 Delair Road as the site of the new church.

In July 1988, Rev. Livingstone Chen accepted a call from a Chinese church in Richmond. Consequently, the Zion church had no pastor for one and a half years until Rev. Steve Jung came out of retirement to act as interim pastor beginning January 1990. Meanwhile, the Search Committee looked for the next pastor. Under God's guidance, Rev. Paul Lam from Hongkong accepted the call and moved to Canada with his family at the end of July 1990.

In the meantime, the ground-breaking ceremony for the new church building took place April 1, 1990. Because of inclement weather, actual construction did not begin until the end of May. The entire project was completed in mid-January 1991 and the Dedication Ceremony was held on January 27, 1991. After almost 12 years, the Zion church can finally worship and serve the Lord in their own building. To God be the glory!

In April 1991, the Zion Christian Reformed Church changed its name to the Zion Chinese Christian Reformed Church. This congregation uses three main languages: Cantonese, Mandarin and English. The following is its schedule of activities:

Sunday Worship 10:30 AM; Sunday School 9:00 AM; Children Worship 10:30 AM; Bible Study Wednesday, 7:30 PM; Mandarin Fellowship Friday, 7:30 PM; Joshua Fellowship (Adult) every 3rd Sunday 1:00 PM; Chinese School Saturday, 9:30 PM.

We extend our warmest welcome to everyone in the community.

12. Grace Evangelical Bible Church

Late in 1945 a group of Evangelical Mennonite Brethren members from the Saskatchewan churches in Dalmeny and Langham, who had moved to this area, met for prayer and discussed their desire to establish an EMB church in Abbotsford.

They had prayer meetings every Sunday afternoon to seek the Lord's will. Abe Warkentin, Art Pankratz and A. A. Dickman were chosen to take the lead. Rev. G. S. Rempel met with them during a visit and served as chairman of the initial committee. The movement quickly gained momentum and outside interest began to grow.

Services were first held in this building on Morey Road

When children began to come, a Sunday School was started. They rented the North Poplar School which soon proved inadequate. Then they moved to a Community Hall on Clearbrook Road. During this time of testing they met for special prayer and discussion. About 20 persons were present and claimed Psalm 50:10–12, believing that God would provide.

On October 20, 1946, under the direction of Rev. A. P. Toews, the District Superintendent of the EMB Conference at that time, the Grace Church of Abbotsford, with 27 charter members, was organized and the building dedicated.

Most of the charter members were from the Langham district in Saskatchewan. Since they had no minister, the committee was responsible to get a speaker for each Sunday. The following ministers of the Conference served from time to time and when they were invited: Rev. G. S. Rempel, Rev. H. R. Harms, Rev. J. N. Wall, and Rev. H. H. Dyck. Ministers from several neighbouring churches kindly helped as they were able.

In 1948 deacon Henry Martens was sent to the Annual Convention to seek a pastor. Subsequently, Rev. C. A. Wall became the first pastor of Grace Church. Since the small group was unable to provide full support,

People arrive for the worship service, 1946

he had to take a part-time secular job to make ends meet. He served faithfully until 1954 and did much visitation.

In 1948, after two rent-free years, the house was filled to capacity. A new piece of property was acquired on Busby Street for $1,400.00. A basement, built mostly by voluntary labour, was dedicated to the Lord in the fall of 1948. It was estimated that the basement would be adequate for 10 years, but after 5 years it was filled. Construction of a proper church building was undertaken and finished in 1953.

The first missionary from Grace Church was Miss Elsie Pankratz who went to Cuba in 1949 and is still serving there with her husband, Don Elliott. Today, over 20 missionaries and missionary families have been sent out from Grace Church. They serve the Lord under a variety of mission agencies in nine different countries.

The vision for a growing ministry led the congregation to purchase new property in the early 70's for the development of a modern church facility. A new building was erected on McMillan Road in the growing eastern area of Abbotsford and was dedicated in 1975. This facility houses

New home of Grace Church, 1953

Grace Evangelical Bible Church and congregation, 2087 McMillan Road

a variety of ministries which reach out to the community at large as well as supporting the ministry of our missionaries around the world.

The pastors of Grace Church who faithfully served the Lord over the years are: Rev. C. A. Wall, Rev. H. P. Wiebe, Dr. John R. Dyck, Rev. H. P. Fast, Rev. Sam H. Epp, Rev. Ken Quiring, Rev. Lyle Wahl, Rev. Mel Koop, Rev. Dwain Holsapple. A number of associate pastors have contributed to the ministry of the church in various areas of specialization.

In July 1987 the delegate body at the Annual Convention of the Evangelical Mennonite Brethren Conference voted overwhelmingly to change the name of the conference to the Fellowship of Evangelical Bible Churches. The congregation of Grace Church supported this change because the overall ministry of both the church and the conference were characterized less by ethnic distinctives and more by outreach to the community at large.

The continuing purpose of Grace Church of Abbotsford is "To provide Biblically balanced fellowship which equips individuals to actively minister in outreach, mutual caring and instruction leading to spiritual maturity."

13. ABBOTSFORD EVANGELICAL FREE CHURCH
"A Worshipping and Caring Church Family"

The Evangelical Free Church of Canada is an independent association of over 120 churches and a partner with other Free Churches worldwide. The name of the denomination identifies its commitment to the inerrancy and authority of Scripture and to its open communion table and congregational form of church government. "Believers only, but all believers," has long been the hallmark of the Evangelical Free Church.

The Abbotsford Evangelical Free Church had its beginning in the heart of Rev. David Enarson. In 1958, while Superintendent of the Canadian Pacific District of the Evangelical Free Church of America, he recognized the need and opportunity for a Free Church in the growing Abbotsford area. The new work was authorized at the District's Silver Anniversary Conference in 1960.

The church began, as many Free Churches have, as a cottage ministry in the homes of interested people. It was officially organized in April 1962, and almost immediately the new congregation purchased one and one third acres near the intersection of Marshall Road and Ware Street. The existing residence on the property was the initial meeting place and David Enarson was the first pastor.

Three months after the official organization, the charter membership of 31 believers was set apart in a Communion service. The following

Abbotsford Evangelical Free Church, early 1960

Sunday the sod was turned for the new building. The structure was built primarily by volunteer labour in 65 days for less than $11,000. It was dedicated on December 2, 1962.

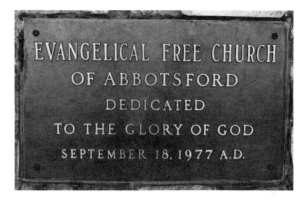

Also in 1962, the Abbotsford EFC began an association with a fledgling junior college in Langley, B.C. From a humble beginning with 17 students, Trinity Western University, an Evangelical Free Church institution, has grown to become a fully accredited university offering both under-graduate and graduate programs.

Over the next 10 years "Abby Free" grew steadily. The sanctuary and other facilities became cramped, calling once again for "cottage ministries" in homes to accommodate the Sunday School overflow.

Building plans for a new, much larger sanctuary were officially launched in May, 1975 and completed two years later. The former sanctuary was renovated to become a library/meeting room and offices.

David Enarson was succeeded in the pastorate by A.H. Pohl (1963–1965), Bill Leschied (1965), Don Danielson (1966–1971), Tim Seim (1971–1978), and Dean Johnson (1978–1990). The present pastor is Rev. Michael (Mike) Adams. He, his wife, Janell and their children arrived on Canada Day, 1991 to begin their ministry. Pastor Mike is assisted by a

Pastoral Staff from left to right: Bob Cottrill, Youth Pastor; Mike Adams, Senior Pastor; Leona Madland, Visitation Coordinator; Tracy Morris, Secretary

Abbotsford Evangelical Free Church, 33218 Marshall Road

Youth Pastor, Bob Cottrill, and a Visitation Coordinator, Leona Madland. The church is served by a full-time secretary, Tracy Morris.

Over the years the growth in both participants and facilities has enabled the church to expand its ministry. The average attendance at morning worship services in 1991 was 307. More than 180 individuals are active members. The present programs include a vibrant Youth Group for high school students and a Pioneer Clubs program for children aged 3–12 which is bursting at the seams. A support group offering friendship and teaching to single mothers was begun in the spring of 1990 and continues to be effective. Two adult groups, "Fifty-Plus" and "Keenagers," are well attended and meet needs for encouragement and friendship among the participants. A network of "House-churches" is being organized under the direction of the Elder for Enfolding.

The support of missions both at home and abroad has always held a high priority in the life of "Abby Free." In its first year as an organized body, the church contributed 17% of its income to missions. In 1991, the church dispersed 31% of its income to the support of 32 missionary families and organizations. Twice, the church has "mothered" new congregations: in Mission (1982), and in Aldergrove (1985).

Matsqui's centennial year is the 30th Anniversary year of the Abbotsford EFC. A celebration of thanks to God is being planned. This milestone will be used to launch another building program as the church is once again at maximum capacity.

It is the strong desire of the Abbotsford Evangelical Free Church to bring glory to God by making disciples of Jesus Christ (Matthew 28:19) in the Fraser Valley and around the world.

14. Matsqui Lutheran Church

During the 1890's, prior to the establishment of the Matsqui Lutheran Church, services were held in various farm homes, with a circuit-rider pastor from Anneiville, B.C., or from the United States. Records include the baptism of a child in 1892.

By 1901, settlers of Scandinavian descent had come from Minnesota, North Dakota and Washington to develop land on Matsqui Prairie. Many of the rich farms in the area are still managed by their descendants. The only road was a trail which later became Riverside Road.

Early Sunday School class

The first meeting of immigrants desiring to establish a Lutheran congregation was held July 5, 1903, at the home of Mr. & Mrs. Martin Kvelsrud. Those who attended included Thomas Jensen, Victor Jensen, Martin Kvelsrud, Carl Lunde, Knute Lunde, Jens Igeland and E. E. Olson, who led in Scripture and prayer. Two week later, they began Sunday school classes at 2 PM, in the Matsqui school.

At the second meeting, Goshen Evangelical Lutheran Norwegian congregation of Matsqui was chosen as the name. Rev. Eric E. Eriksen of Whatcom County, Washington was appointed as the first temporary pastor. He was paid $60 a year plus special offerings taken at Christmas and Pentecost. He was followed by Rev. John Quale on October 18, 1904. Land for a church was donated by Mr. and Mrs. G. A. Halvorson and construction began in 1904.

After Rev. Quale passed away while still a young man, the congregation was again served by visiting pastors. Rev. Benjamin Sand became pastor on October 14, 1906, with a salary of $125 per year. The first janitor was paid 15 cents a Sunday, according to minutes of January 19, 1907. Anna Nelson, the first organist, received an annual salary of $10.

Other pastors were Rev. O. Skattebol, who took charge May 24, 1911; Rev. K. O. Elliassen, December 26, 1913; Rev. L. A. Mathre, October 19, 1917; and Rev. Olaf Borge, January 23, 1918.

Although the building was erected in 1904, the church was not entirely finished until 1920. Dedication of the church was a special feature of the three-day district conference held in Matsqui in 1920. Visiting pastors, delegates and guests from U.S. and Canada were housed by members of the congregation. The ladies aid rented Matsqui hall and served noon and evening meals there. Also in 1920, the congregation changed its name to Goshen Evangelical Lutheran Church.

First resident pastor, Rev. Kandal, with confirmation class of 1946

Through the efforts of the ladies aid, a church parlour was built in 1925 on the lot adjoining the church. Money was raised by holding bazaars, quilting "bees," turkey dinners and other similar affairs.

On January 25, 1925, Rev. Norby became the pastor, followed by Rev. H. Holtus March 5, 1925, Rev. C. B. Johansen January 13, 1926; Rev. E. Torgerson October 12, 1933; Rev. R. Anderson January 4, 1939; Rev. A. M. Eggen, January 7, 1942 and Rev. A. H. Solheim, June 2, 1945. In response to a petition to the president of Home Missions, Rev. K. O. Kandal was installed as the first resident pastor on August 2, 1945.

The Fraser River flood of 1948 damaged the church facilities extensively. With the help of the Flood Aid fund, Red Cross, Kinsmen, local businesses, the ladies aid, the congregation and assistance from other Canadian and U.S. churches, both church and parlour were restored. The church was moved closer to the parlour and the room formed by connecting the two was used for the young people. A furnace, hot and cold water and kitchen cupboards were added. Rev. Kandal directed the work on the church and officiated at the dedication ceremony June 26, 1949.

Charter members, Mrs. A. C. Gustafson and Mrs. Pauline Igeland with Rev. Kandal, planting a magnolia tree after the 1948 flood

By March, 1953, the church was self-supporting and the name had been changed to Matsqui Evangelical Lutheran Church. On July 26, 1953, the church celebrated its golden jubilee, with Dr. J. R. Lavik as guest speaker.

With the death of Rev. Kandal in January 1955, the church was left without a pastor. Mr. O. Lokken served until Rev. M. Knudsen was installed in August, 1955. Mt. Calvary congregation in Mission was organized in 1956 under

Pastor Arne Jensen

his guidance and he served both congregations until May, 1961. Pastor S. J. Rude served as interim pastor until Rev. Daniel J. Vinge, began his work in December, 1962.

A parsonage to serve both congregations was built in 1959 adjacent to the Mission church. In 1962 the church parlours were expanded, providing overflow space for the sanctuary. Another room was added and dedicated at the diamond anniversary service April 29, 1963.

On July 18, 1965 Dr. J. Wilch was installed to serve both Matsqui Lutheran Church and Peace Lutheran Church in Abbotsford. Rev. V. Roste followed on July 21, 1968, serving both Matsqui and Mission. In February, 1972, the congregation asked national church officials for a student intern pastor, as a step toward gaining a full-time pastor to serve the single congregation of Matsqui Evangelical Lutheran Church.

During its 70th anniversary year, Rev. O. H. Olson of Edmonton was installed July 29, 1972. Rev. John Neumann served the parish from 1976–80, until his sudden death. Through his foresight and personal conviction, the church opened its facilities to groups ministering to those seeking spiritual help and guidance.

Rev. Paul Phillips served as interim pastor until Rev. Arne Jensen, a former chaplain at federal prisons in Agassiz and Mission, was installed in 1982.

During this Matsqui centennial year, Matsqui Lutheran Church will hold a commemorative service on Sunday, Sept. 13 at 3 p.m. Guest speakers will be Bishop Marlin Aadland of the Evangelical Lutheran Church of Canada, and Mayor Dave Kandal, son of the first resident pastor. A banquet will follow the service.

"Unless the Lord builds the house, those who build it labour in vain." May we continue to be an active worshipping community in Matsqui village.

Wanda Kemprud

Matsqui Evangelical Lutheran Church

15. Peace Lutheran Church

The history of Peace Lutheran Church spans a period of 56 years, beginning in 1936 when six Lutheran families gathered for devotional services in homes. These services were occasionally conducted by the Rev. J. Fritz of Christ Lutheran Church in Chilliwack.

When the group grew too large to be accommodated in homes, worship services were conducted in the basement of Trinity United Church, Abbotsford, for ten years. By 1946, Pastor R. Mensch of Chilliwack was conducting regular services twice a month and the name Peace Lutheran Church had been adopted.

The first worshippers with Pastor Fritz (center)

By 1950 the congregation had grown as a result of immigration from Europe and began to search for property on which to build a church. In October 1955, a site at the corner of Ware and Marshall Roads was purchased for $1,800.00. The former Mennonite Brethren Bible School on Huntingdon Road was purchased for $1,350.00 and moved in two sections to the Ware Road location. The building was renovated through the cooperative efforts of men and women, both young and old. Later, a bell tower, basement and parsonage were added.

On July 8, 1956 the congregation celebrated the first worship service in its own facility. On October 28, 1956, Peace Lutheran Church was dedicated to the glory of God in a service of praise and thanksgiving conducted by Dr. K. Holfeld, president of the Evangelical Lutheran Church of Canada.

The Rev. Alvin Miller was the first full-time resident pastor, serving from July 1957 until June 1962. A total of six full-time and nine interim pastors have served the congregation from 1946 to 1992. The present pas-

First church building, 1956

tor, the Rev. Adolf Manz was installed on May 1, 1983. On December 17, 1989, Miss Gertie Gatzke became the first parish worker at Peace Lutheran Church.

In 1980 a new building was begun and completed in 1982 with much volunteer labour by members of the congregation. A mortgage burning celebration was held in December 1989, and the official 35th Anniversary was commemorated in May 1990.

Peace Lutheran Church remains a bilingual congregation, conducting weekly services in both the German and the English languages. Some of the German speaking members are charter members of the congregation.

The ministry of Peace Lutheran Church includes Sunday School from nursery to grade seven, Adult Bible Studies and a Prayer Group, Youth Group and Junior Youth, Pioneer Clubs, Young Adults and a Mother's Support Group. A New Horizons group (Peace Golden Friendship Club) and an Alcoholics Anonymous group also meet at Peace Lutheran Church on a regular basis.

The Mission Statement of Peace Lutheran Church describes the identity and purpose of this congregation:

"As God's chosen people, and empowered by the Holy Spirit, the members of Peace Lutheran Church seek to strengthen the ministry of worship, witness, education and service through the proclamation of the Gospel and the administration of the Sacraments to our own congregation, as well as reaching out with the love of Jesus Christ to our community and into the world.

As members of Peace Lutheran Church, we are called
- to be witnesses of God's love,
- to live as God's faithful people,
- to hear and learn God's word,
- to share God's Supper.

We are called to bear witness to God's love,
- to proclaim the Good News of God in Christ through word and deed,
- to serve all people, following the example of our Lord, Jesus,
- to strive for justice and peace in all the earth.

Ida Hood

Peace Lutheran Church, 2029 Ware Road

16. TRINITY LUTHERAN CHURCH

The history of Trinity Lutheran Church is a story of the faithfulness of a great God to a humble people who were faithful to Him.

In spring 1930, at the request of Mr. Chris Zurowski, monthly Lutheran services led by Rev. V. Meyer from Vancouver, were held in the McAdam home on Vye Road. That winter Rev. A. Haake, from the New Westminster parish, took over the work. By 1934, he listed 24 souls and 11 communicant members. Those numbers may seem rather small now, but the Abbotsford area was very small in the 1930's.

By 1935 this group of Lutheran believers aligned themselves with the Chilliwack parish which had recently installed a new pastor. For the next five years, Rev. R. F. Holtzen ministered to the Abbotsford group as well. For three years services were held in the F. Roust home on Nelson Road. During 1938, they worshipped on the second floor of the "Hambley Hatchery," located on the northeast corner of Essendene Avenue and the Abbotsford–Mission Highway. In 1939, services were again moved to private homes: first the H. Bosch home, then the C. Zurowski home. For 11 years, beginning in 1941, services were conducted at the J. C. Ast home on McKenzie Road. In 1945 the Fraser Valley parish was split and Abbotsford became its own parish with weekly services.

Following Rev. Holtzen, Abbotsford was served by Rev. A. Riep (1940–42), Rev. Fred T. Gabert (1942–45), Rev. Alfred E. Enders (1945–46) and Rev. M. A. Cohrs (1946–54). In 1952, after many years of conducting services in private homes, the congregation rented a larger facility: the Annex Hall of St. Matthews Anglican Church, then located on Montvue Avenue, a half block south of S. Fraserway. The church was thankful to be worshipping in proper facilities even though they were shared with the Anglican Church as well as a Boy Scout Troop. Two years later Rev. Cohrs resigned and was succeeded by Rev. H. S. Fox who served us from the Chilliwack parish.

During the three years that the Abbotsford Lutheran parish worshipped in the Anglican Hall, God led us to formally organize the Abbotsford congregation, officially named Trinity Lutheran Church. What an exciting time it must have been when twelve charter members signed our constitution. They were S. Wagner, J. Geberdt, E. Zurowski, J. C. Ast, H. Schulz, W. Froese, O. Zurowski, A. Haglund, C. Haglund, D.G.B. Dyck, J. Hunter & Rev. H. S. Fox. It is interesting to note that of these twelve charter members, two are still active in Trinity Lutheran:

Jack Hunter and David Dyck. Furthermore, three of the charter families: Zurowski, Ast and Dyck, are still represented at Trinity Lutheran.

In quick succession, a lot was purchased at the corner of Cherry Street and Marshall Road and plans were laid to construct a church building. In 1955, as we looked forward to having our own church, we temporarily moved services to the dining room of Jack & Jill Restaurant on the Abbotsford–Mission Highway.

Trinity Lutheran Church, 1957

In the summer of 1956 Trinity's first full-time worker, student-pastor Rudy Nast arrived. During his year with us, our new building was constructed under the supervision of Mr. Ted Galvitz (a member of Trinity), with abundant volunteer labour. With great thankfulness, the church was dedicated to the glory of God on July 28, 1957. The next month Rev. Mark Misch from the seminary in Minnesota became our first resident pastor. He arrived in Abbotsford alone and after serving for eight years, left with a wife (Marie) and a family. Beginning in 1964, Rev. Herb Fruson and his family faithfully ministered for 13 years and taught us to grow in our faith. In 1979, Rev. Bob Schulze began his work in our congregation.

Over the past 62 years God has richly blessed the ministry of Trinity Lutheran Church in Abbotsford. Many people have come to faith in Jesus Christ, acknowledging Him as their Lord and Saviour. Hundreds have been baptized, confirmed, married and buried, their lives touched by the caring Christian pastors and members who have given much that the Word of God might be proclaimed.

During the ministry of Pastor Bob, Trinity grew, making it necessary to consider new and larger facilities. In 1984, a property was purchased at 3845 Gladwin Road. That year, a second full-time church worker, Mr. Harold Rust arrived to serve as director of parish ministries. During his three years with us, Harold exhibited a special love for our young people. On May 31, 1987, the last worship service was conducted in our beloved Cherry Street Church. Since it had been sold to the Salvation Army, we again moved to temporary facilities as we waited for the completion of our new church building.

Trinity Lutheran Church, 3845 Gladwin

On February 14, 1988, we sang "To God Be The Glory" as we dedicated our new church to His glory and service. That year we welcomed Mr. Craig Cooper for a one year posting as director of parish ministries. In 1989 Rev. Rudy Pastucha began service in the areas of youth work and evangelism.

At present, we hold three worship services each week:

Sunday   8:30 AM (9:45 AM Sunday School & Adult Bible Studies)
           11:00 AM
Thursday   7:00 PM

The ministry of our church is very broad and offers areas of involvement for almost everyone. A variety of weekly adult Bible studies are under way as well as opportunities for involvement with youth or young adults. Our large, active "Nifty Fifty Plus" group meets Thursday mornings.

Trinity Lutheran Church believes itself to be a friendly and caring community church with a love for mission work. Through our affiliation with Lutheran Church Canada we strongly support mission work locally, nationally and internationally. Trinity helps to sponsor "The Lutheran Hour" broadcast on CFVR. Each February, the Lutheran School of Evangelism, with participants from across Canada, is conducted in our facilities. It features powerful Lutheran speakers and teachers who help equip pastors and lay people to effectively witness and evangelize in their own communities.

17. The Church of God in Christ Mennonite

In the latter half of the nineteenth century political changes in Russia deeply affected the Mennonites. Among them was a small group in the Molotschna area of the Ukraine who held to the basic tenets of the Anabaptist faith, particularly conscientious objection to military service. Fearing the loss of this principle, they migrated en masse to North America in 1873–74, some settling in Canada and some in the mid-western States. The Church of God in Christ Mennonite in the Fraser Valley has its roots in that migration.

Through the years, this group lost one basic ingredient in their religion, the concept of the 'new birth.' A few years after their arrival in Manitoba, John Holdeman, a minister from Ohio came and preached salvation by personal faith in Christ. A large segment of the group experienced salvation and were rebaptized. This was the beginning of the Church of God in Christ, Mennonite, (sometimes called Holdeman), in Canada.

From Manitoba, these people and their descendants moved outward to new horizons. In 1950 a nucleus formed a small congregation in the Fraser Valley. The first church was located on Mt. Lehman Road, half a

Church of God in Christ, Downes & Ross Roads

mile north of Highway 1, with Frank Wiebe as minister. They outgrew the church and built a new one at the corner of Ross and Downes Roads in 1959. This building, with an added Sunday school wing, is still in use.

A denomination-wide conference in 1974 recommended that all our children be afforded the opportunity to attend private Christian schools. In 1976 our congregation began one class at the Junior High level. Before long the elementary school grades were added. The Sunday school facilities were renovated to accommodate the school. Our goals for our children have been realized fairly well. They get an education acceptable to the Department of Education. We are grateful for the support we receive from the department.

Being an agriculturally oriented people, most early adherents who moved here settled on poultry and fruit farms. Others laboured carpentry, mechanics, trucking and related industries. As times have changed, so have work patterns.

We believe in practical outreach. The Valhaven Home on Sunset Avenue off Mt. Lehman Road, a facility for senior citizens, consisting of 26 beds and four self-help units, forms part of this outreach. An active Sewing Circle distributes quilts and other items to various causes, including layettes to needy mothers in the MSA Hospital. Once a month, members of the congregation, particularly the youth, have a singing outreach. Groups visit various facilities for the elderly. Jail visitation is promoted. Children from the community attend our Summer Vacation Bible school. Personal witnessing is encouraged and a viable tract ministry maintained. Our congregation heartily contributes to the worldwide mission and relief program of our conference. A local Christian Disaster Relief program is activated when a need arises.

Our ministers and deacons are elected out of the congregation and ordained to their office. We presently have two ministers and one deacon. The gift of 'helps' is also encouraged.

We maintain certain practices that may differentiate us from others. We strongly oppose the use and ownership of televisions and radios. We believe in a simple lifestyle. Espousing 1 Cor. 11, our women wear devotional head-coverings, a symbol of God's order in creation.

We believe that the Bible is the infallible Word of God, that Jesus Christ is verily God's Son and the Holy Spirit is "God with us." We accept the 33 Articles of Faith as promulgated at Dortrecht, Holland by the Anabaptists in the 16th century. We believe that the general conference of the church holds the right to give its members direction for practical Christian living.

Persons are baptized only when they have personally experienced repentance and have accepted Christ as Saviour and Lord. At baptism they vow to be true to God and the Church as the body of Christ as long as they live. If a member breaks this covenant he forfeits his right to the fellowship of the church and communion. Upon repentance and renewal of his vows he is reinstated into full fellowship.

Ministers from other areas in the conference teach and preach at open services during our annual evangelistic meetings. This time of renewal and ingathering is climaxed by a communion service.

You are cordially invited to services at our church at the corner of Downes and Ross on Sunday morning. See you there!

18. Clearbrook Mennonite Church

HISTORICAL SKETCH

Early in 1952, a group of believers of the Mennonite faith reached the conclusion that the Clearbrook area needed another German-speaking church. Clearbrook Realty donated a piece of land at 32027 Peardonville Road. With much volunteer help, especially from the West Abbotsford Mennonite Church, the building was begun and completed within the calendar year. David Falk, Corn. Kehler and the Service Committee assumed responsibility for the building process.

On December 8, 1952, the Clearbrook Mennonite Church was organized under the leadership of Rev. Abram Loewen, with a membership of 60. The first deacons were Cornelius Wall, H. Sawatzky and Fr. Derksen. During the early years, Elder J. B. Wiens of Vancouver often served at communion or baptism.

A number of persons ministered here during the past 40 years: Abram Loewen from 1952 to 1957, Elder Hugo Scheffler 1957–1962, Rev. J. L. Zacharias 1963, Elder J. J. Sawatsky 1964–1972. Elder J. C. Schmidt assumed leadership in 1972, but retired due to illness. Upon recovery, he assisted with preaching and visitation until he went to be with the Lord on February 2, 1978. Then Elder Jacob Enns assumed spiritual leadership

Clearbrook Mennonite Church

Ministers Walter Thielmann, Peter Harms, P.J. Froese, Jacob Enns

until 1987, though he continues to help in preaching and visitation wherever possible. Rev. Peter Harms served as leader in 1988 and is still active. Rev. George Groening served as interim pastor in 1989. Rev. Walter Thielmann assumed the pastorate in December, 1989.

Various people have served in elected offices over the years. Presently, the following brethren serve as deacons: Jacob Dyck, Peter Rempel, Dietrich Krause and Peter Koop. Sunday School superintendents have included Rev. Is. Epp, Herm. Janzen, P. Martens, Bill Janzen, Jacob Dyck, Peter Rempel, Peter I. Dyck, J. J. Sawatsky and presently Jacob Dyck. Moderators in recent years have included Bill Janzen, Peter Rempel, Jacob Dyck, C. P. Kehler and now, Jacob Brucks.

The Ladies Aids served throughout the history of the church, under the capable leadership of people like Mrs. A. Loewen, Mrs. H. Scheffler, Mrs. A. Enns, Mrs. M. Klassen, Mrs. B. Janzen, Miss Tina Plett and presently, Mrs. Martha Krause.

A highlight in our church history was the celebration of our 25th year anniversary. On September 2, 1977, together with friends from neighbouring churches, we gathered at the church for thanksgiving and praise, honouring our heavenly Father for the mercy and grace He bestowed on us during the 25 years we have been able to worship here with other Christians.

OUR PURPOSE AND REASON FOR EXISTENCE

We, the Clearbrook Mennonite Church, see a great need to minister to the elderly, aged and sick, mainly in the German language. At a time

Sunday School teachers at Clearbrook Mennonite

when the younger generation is moving forward fast, we feel it is also necessary to look back and see what has been done in the past, to recognize those who were involved, and in thankfulness, serve those who are still with us to the best of our ability. Recently, more and more older people have joined our church, so that most of our present 160 members are over 60 years of age.

The emphasis in our church life includes worship, evangelism and fellowship. Our greatest witness to our community is the power of prayer. We also support Mennonite Conference projects as well as MCC and missions financially.

In the foreseeable future our projections are to serve those who need us and especially encourage attendance in our recently established children's Sunday School.

19. Eben–Ezer Mennonite Church

The Eben-Ezer Mennonite Church is a spiritual home to about 500 members and their dependents. A walk through the minutes going back to 1963, catalogues the decisions which have shaped the character of Eben-Ezer Mennonite.

Eben-Ezer Mennonite Church, 2051 Windsor Street

On February 4, 1963, 61 members of the Mennonite Church met at the home of John & Mary Bergen and decided to form a new congregation. Jake Siemens was elected chairman and John Krahn secretary. They planned to buy the property at the corner of Windsor and Marshall Roads. The building committee consisted of J. Redekop Sr., J. Wall, J. Hildebrandt, W. Thiessen and P. Krause. Rev. J. Tilitzky was called to lead this congregation, while Rev. Henry Neudorf was asked to assist as a minister. Two weeks later, the group agreed to call itself "Eben-Ezer Mennonite Church in Abbotsford". Sod turning for the construction of the church was held February 27, 1963 and the dedication of the building took place July 14. On March 4, 1963 Isaak & Mika Bergen were elected as the first deacon couple.

Communion

Music ministry

During the following year, the Sunday School wing was added and dedicated Dec. 13, 1964.

In November, 1965, Eben-Ezer decided to give full financial support to missionaries Peter & Lydia Kehler in Taiwan.

By a large majority, the church voted to join the M.E.I. Society in April 1968.

On May 12, 1970 we decided to extend the church on the north side.

In March, 1963 Rev. Tilitzky was granted a 6 months study leave. Rev. H.J.Neudorf took charge of the spiritual ministry. Henry Paetkau from Ontario was hired as youth pastor.

In April, 1977 Rev. Bruno Epp was called as leading minister. A year later, we hired Harry Loewen as church worker for youth and music.

In 1980, 40 members agreed to start a new church, Emmanuel.

Children's Feature

In March, 1981 Rev. Arnold Fast was called as Interim Pastor, until Rev. J. Tilitzky was asked to serve as leading minister in May, 1981.

In January, 1982 the youth suggested that the church consider the addition of a gym. A year later, the construction was approved as soon as

$100,000 had been given or pledged.

In May 1982, Anne Giesbrecht was hired as full-time youth and music director. Early in 1983, Jake Friesen became a third paid worker, (¾ time), with duties in Christian Education,

Ministry to seniors

preaching, visitations and assistant to the leading minister. In August, 1983, Dave Kropp joined the staff as full-time youth worker.

On February 17, 1986 Eben-Ezer called Herman Stahl for college and Careers and educational work, and his wife Marilse Rempel Stahl as music and choir director.

On April 28, 1986, it was agreed in principle, to consider changing the format of the Sunday morning worship service. In June it was agreed to try a new church service with English & German messages more separated. By January, 1987 a substantial majority voted in favour of continuing our Sunday services as introduced earlier on a trial basis.

Eben-Ezer Mennonite Church celebrated its 25th Anniversary on June 24–25, 1988. The church continues to enjoy the blessings of the heavenly Father. The two Sunday worship services in the morning and one in the afternoon are geared to the needs of Christians from a variety of age groups and backgrounds: German, Canadian, and Laotian.

Laotian Christian Church, sponsored at Eben-Ezer by CMinBC and Eben-Ezer, beginning in the early 1980's

20. EMMANUEL MENNONITE CHURCH

Emmanuel Mennonite Church, 3471 Clearbrook Road, was conceived in the late 1970's when some members of the Eben-Ezer Mennonite Church had the vision to plant a new church because the latter was over-crowded and because of the need to establish an English-speaking church. On March 26, 1980 a group of interested members met to discuss the possibilities. A five-member Planning Committee was appointed to formulate long range goals.

Eben-Ezer graciously per-mitted the group to meet in her facilities for the remainder of the year, on alternate Sunday evenings. The early meetings were devoted to prayer for unity, love, wisdom, and a pos-sible pastor.

On September 21, 1980 39 people expressed their faith by signing an official membership list. Two months later, they chose the name Emmanuel Mennonite Church.

Ground-breaking ceremony

On December 28, 1980 Eben-Ezer had a moving farewell for its departing members and then on January 4, 1981 Emmanuel Mennonite Church had her first Sunday morning service in the rented chapel of First Memorial Services on Mt. Lehman Road. The 120 seat facility was

Emmanuel Mennonite Church, 3471 Clearbrook Road

packed as Conference Minister Jake Tilitzky spoke on "The Ingredients of Success." Two months later the congregation moved to the former Peardonville Church building on Huntingdon Road, which more adequately accommodated the growing needs.

Pastor David Ortis

A major step of faith was taken on January 19, 1981 with the decision to purchase a 3½ acre parcel of land in the heart of a rapidly growing subdivision on Clearbrook Road. On August 30 the sod-turning ceremony took place, and on November 28 of the following year the congregation moved in.

Services were conducted in the activity area until the sanctuary was completed in late 1984.

Gene Klassen was installed as pastor of Emmanuel on May 24, 1981 with Dick Rempel officiating. After three years the church accepted his letter of resignation and Ron Toews, a professional counsellor, was hired on an interim basis until David Ortis assumed pastoral duties on August 1, 1986. Peter Goertzen served as youth pastor on a half-time basis until Carl Adrian was hired full-time in 1990.

From the outset, Emmanuel was a young congregation. The over fifties group was missing entirely. Services informal, encouraging participation of all ages. Many took the opportunity to the share their faith journeys. Care Groups were established to provide an intimate setting for Bible study, prayer, sharing and caring.

Over the years growth has happened in a variety of ways. In addition to the regular proclamation of the Word and the fellowship of believers, some unique experiences have also moulded Emmanuel. Some were tragic, such as the untimely deaths of five children over a couple of years. Others were miraculous, such as the reunification of the Nguyen family, five

Care Group Leaders, 1982

Vietnamese "boat people" whom Emmanuel sponsored.

The people of Emmanuel continue to worship God, to teach and to preach, but they also corporately minister to specific community needs. That is why the Open Door, a ministry to single moms, was founded in 1991. Currently, Lori Bahnman, the branch coordinator, gives leadership to the joint effort of four local churches to help single moms find love, acceptance, and hope. Countless people have provided child-care, cooked meals, lead Bible Studies, and arranged comfortable settings for friendship and caring.

The Nguyen Family, 1990

Open Door Ministry

The Central Valley Academy of Music, which served about 275 musicians a week, also has its home in the Emmanuel Mennonite Church.

As the people of Emmanuel look into the future they want to claim the promise that the name suggests, "God with us." As God has been present in the past, He will be present in the future.

Worship Service at Emmanuel Mennonite Church

21. Olivet Mennonite Church

Olivet Mennonite Church, at 2630 Langdon Street in Clearbrook, has been a part of the Abbotsford–Matsqui community since its charter in 1960. It is affiliated with the Conference of Mennonites in B.C., the Conference of Mennonites in Canada, and the General Conference Mennonite Church.

Conceived as an English-speaking church which would be an outreach to the community, Olivet began with a group of 52 charter members, coming mainly from the Clearbrook Mennonite Church in late 1959. Ground was broken for the church building on Langdon Street in November 1960, and the young fellowship moved into the building in May 1961. The church has been added onto and remodeled several times over its three decades:

Commitment before construction

Olivet Mennonite Church, 2630 Langdon

MISSIONS

Mission emphasis at Olivet

the upper sanctuary in December 1963, the education wing in 1972 and enlargement of the sanctuary in 1980. Much of the work during these construction and renovation phases was done by volunteers from the congregation.

Olivet has enjoyed a diversity of members throughout the years. Young families, those in the middle years, and the retired comprise the congregation today. Members have pursued a variety of careers ranging from farming to business, from the trades to the professions.

Backgrounds too, vary: many members are native to B.C., others have moved here from different provinces. Some were born in Russia and a few have immigrated from other countries.

Volunteerism and service have always been strengths of Olivet people. Several dozen have given voluntary service in Canada and the United States, and about two dozen have been involved in overseas mission and relief work in Africa, Asia and South America.

Here at home, Olivet members continue to volunteer their services at the Mennonite Central Committee (MCC) store and other places in the community.

Throughout the years, a number of pastors have ably served the congregation. Henry D. Penner was the first pastor, from 1960 to 1966. Abe Buhler ministered from 1967–75. Henry C. Born served as interim pastor from 1975–77, until David P. Neufeld began as senior pastor in 1977. Following his death in 1982, associate pastor Lowell Gerber served as leading pas-

Ladies minister with sewing skills

tor until Art Willms assumed the leadership role 1983–86. Lowell Gerber (1986–88) and Henry Born (1988–90) each served in the interim until the current pastor, Peter Penner, began his ministry in January 1991.

Associate pastors have included Bob Schmidt, Vernon Reimer, Neil Matthies (music, outreach, youth), Linda Buhler Peters (music), H. T. Klassen, Lowell Gerber, Henry Unrau and Erwin Klassen (youth).

Today, Olivet offers something for all ages and interests. Choirs, boys' and girls' clubs, Sunday school, women's auxiliaries, youth groups, young adult fellowships and home Bible studies are all part of the life of the congregation as it seeks to serve God in the larger community.

The current membership of Olivet Mennonite Church is 309.

Children participate in Olivet worship service

22. West Abbotsford Mennonite Church

A mong the early Mennonite settlers in the Abbotsford area were those who eventually founded the West Abbotsford Mennonite Church in 1936.

During those early years, Mennonite ministers from Coghlan (Aldergrove) cycled the eight to ten miles to Abbotsford every Sunday to serve the group of believers who met in homes.

Shortly after its founding on December 28, 1936, the church chose Rev. Peter P. Epp as its leading minister, and by April of the next year, struck a committee to plan the building of a church. The municipality donated two acres on the corner of King and Townline Roads, and by the fall of 1937, the sanctuary was under construction. The building measured 24 by 40 feet. Some of the lumber was obtained by dismantling the Mill Lake Lumber Mill. (see photo, Introduction)

Events on the church calendar during the early years included baptism at Pentecost, Vacation Bible School, the Sunday School picnic at Mt. Lehman Park (now Dunach School), Thanksgiving–missions festival and the children's Christmas Eve program. From its inception, this church exercised a congregational form of government.

In 1945, after a number of shorter term ministers, Rev. H.M. Epp, newly arrived from Manitoba, was elected as leading minister. His tenure ushered in a period characterized by strong, stable leadership and dramatic church growth. As leader, he felt responsible for the life of every member and frequently enquired about one's spiritual welfare. His motto was "Holy to the Lord," which he not only taught and preached, but also lived by. He expected church members to do the same.

Very shortly after its founding, the church changed its name to "United Mennonite Church of Abbotsford", to conform to provincial conference expectations. It was changed to the present name in 1950.

The membership grew rapidly during

The "long" West Abbotsford Mennonite Church, 1949.

the early decades. In 1946 it stood at 145; grew to 340 in 1954, and to approximately 450 in 1958. They included settlers from Canada's prairie provinces, post World War II refugees, and a few immigrants from Paraguay and Mexico. To accommodate this rapid growth, the congregation

Rev. H. M. Epp (front, centre), ministers and deacons with 1952 baptismal class

undertook two separate building programs: one in 1946 and the next in 1949, that resulted in the so-called "long church" which was filled to overflowing by 1952. Sunday School attendance peaked at 290 children and 100 youth in 1954.

During the 1950s, two new churches were established to relieve the overcrowding at West Abbotsford. The Clearbrook Mennonite Church at the corner of Clearbrook and Peardonville Roads was organized in 1951. The same year, a group of 15 members founded the Peardonville Mennonite Church at South Aberdeen, where they had established an outreach Sunday School program that year.

Also in 1951 the church's mission and evangelism emphasis resulted in a Sunday School outreach on Sumas Prairie. (See photo in "Prairie Chapel" essay.) Through a vacation Bible School outreach in the Burns Lake area in 1955, Rev. Abe Buhler and Jack Nickel, founded a children's camp known as Ootsa Lake Bible Camp.

Over the years, some 90 members have been involved in voluntary service, either overseas or in North America. Most notably, the Peter Derksens, who were commissioned for overseas service in 1954, are still working in Japan.

Following Rev. Epp's death in 1958, Rev. P.J. Froese was elected leader. During his tenure, the style and language of worship became an issue for members from diverse backgrounds. In 1963 a group established the Eben-Ezer Church.

In 1967–1968, during the search for a new pastor, Rev. H.P. Fast gave interim leadership. Rev. Peter Harms began his three-year ministry in the fall of 1968. He inaugurated the dual worship service — one in German and one in English. His strength lay in his pulpit ministry where he served equally well in both languages.

Rev. Dietrich Rempel came to West Abbotsford Church in 1972. He introduced innovations like women deaconesses and offered "lay people" increasingly visible roles in the worship service. The most notable physical change during his tenure was the construction of a new sanctuary in 1976. During the latter part of his tenure, an assistant to the pastor was introduced to the staff.

Dave Wilson, the assistant to the pastor, became interim leader when Pastor Rempel resigned in 1981. Rev. Paul and MaryAnne Boschman came in October, 1983, and made efforts to meet specific needs and promote missions.

After the Boschmans left West Abbotsford in 1988, Rev. Stan Martens served as interim leader for two years. In September, 1990 the congregation welcomed Rev. David Friesen as leading minister. He and his wife, Doris provide warm and sensitive leadership to our church.

The Christian education program at West Abbotsford includes Sunday School, Vacation Bible School, Boys Club and Girls Club. The local community German School, presently held at the MEI, had its birth in this congregation during the 1940s.

From the beginning, this congregation has been involved in numerous church-related schools. It was the first General Conference Church to join the MEI Society in 1951. It supported the Bethel Bible Institute, located next door, and more recently, Columbia Bible College.

Like any other institution or organization, West Abbotsford has had its share of growing pains as well as blessings. We, who are "earthen vessels", are grateful that the "treasure" is not bound by our weaknesses. God has transcended those weaknesses and empowered us to share the "treasure" with those around us.

West Abbotsford Mennonite Church today, on the original site, 31216 King Road

Introduction to the Mennonite Brethren

The Mennonite Brethren, who trace their theological roots to the Dutch Reformer, Menno Simons (1536), began in 1860 as a renewal movement within the Mennonite Church in Russia. In the 1870's, when the Russian government, supported by the Orthodox Church, began to restrict the privileges of the Protestant churches, many groups including Mennonite Brethren migrated to Canada and U.S.A. Following the Russian Revolution in 1917, and the subsequent anarchy and famine, another wave of Mennonites immigrated to Canada in the 1920's, settling largely in the prairie provinces or Ontario. By the end of the decade, a few Mennonite Brethren settled in the upper Fraser Valley of B.C., specifically Agassiz, Sardis and Yarrow, where they purchased most of the familiar "flat land" available at bargain prices.

Of primary importance to them were spiritual fellowship and opportunities for the Christian education of their children in the compact Yarrow settlement. Thus, in 1928, some 20 families participated in worship services in the local schoolhouse, and on February 3, 1929, organized a church of 96 members. They erected the first church building, dedicating it in Fall, 1930.

When land became scarce in the Yarrow area, Mennonite newcomers purchased "cheap" property in "Poverty Flats", the freshly logged plateau south and west of Abbotsford. Here they erected simple dwellings and cleared the land of stumps. Arable clearings were planted to vegetables and strawberries, for a quick cash crop. Some found work on farms in Sumas Prairie, or local sawmills.

First South Abbotsford Church

On May 1, 1932, these pioneers, under the leadership of the Yarrow congregation, organized the South Abbotsford MB Church with 31 members. In view of the relatively primitive transportation and new families settling northwest of the first congregation in what is now Clearbrook, it was agreed to begin another church. Thus 26 families remained at South Abbotsford, while nine families founded the North

First North Abbotsford MB Church

Abbotsford Church on January 24, 1936, the same year that South Abbotsford began a Bible School (now CBC). In 1944, the MEI, an inter-Mennonite high school, was also conceived at South Abbotsford. (For more details see individual church entries.)

In 1943, the Yarrow MB Church helped to organize another congregation of some eight families on Sumas Prairie, in the new settlement of Arnold.

Meanwhile, MB families from the prairies gravitated to the Matsqui flats and took up dairy farming. South Abbotsford released one of its leading ministers to organize the Matsqui MB Church of 71 members in

MB Bible School at South Abbotsford

1945. At first the congregation met in a converted farmhouse on Riverside Road in Matsqui village, but as more Mennonites bought out the "old-timers," plans for building a church were set in motion and the basement completed to accommodate the growing congregation. The June, 1948, flood completely inundated the church basement. "Some through the water, some through the flood, some through the fire, but all through His blood," was to have historic as well as prophetic significance for the group. Membership peaked around 200 in 1955.

The congregation had a strong emphasis on Christian education, becoming a sponsoring church of MEI, with many students there, as well as the Bible school. The young people, realizing that outreach in the community was handicapped by services conducted only in the German language, taught Vacation Bible Schools in summer and started outreach Sunday schools on Sunday afternoons. In 1958, after the protracted campaign of evangelist George R. Brunk in this area, Matsqui, along with many other MB churches, conducted bilingual services, primarily for the sake of its own young people, and secondarily to encourage outreach.

As older couples retired, almost invariably selling to Dutch immigrant-dairymen, few young people followed their parents' farming tradition. Instead, they went into education, business and trades in more urban set-

Matsqui MB Church 1945–1975

tings. Early in 1959, during a bitterly cold but sunny Sunday morning, the wood-burning furnace overheated and the church burned to the ground. However, while the congregation met temporarily at the Bible School on Clearbrook Road, the church was rebuilt on the old foundation, some modernizations. By 1973, the membership had diminished to 111 and in 1975, the church dissolved, becoming the first extinct MB church in this area. The members joined various MB churches. The building was sold and is now occupied by the Community Baptist Church.

East Aldergrove MB Church

East Aldergrove, a daughter church of Clearbrook, was organized in 1947 with 117 members. Three years later, in 1950, 197 members of South Abbotsford founded the first totally English-language MB church in the area, known as Abbotsford, then McCallum Road MB and later renamed Central Heights, now the largest MB church in the lower Fraser Valley.

Beginning in 1939, with a Vacation Bible school in Bradner, younger people from many MB churches organized outpost Sunday Schools. For example: South Abbotsford sponsored Ruskin (now a Baptist church), South Otter (now Hillside Community Church), as well as Dewdney, Hatzic, Jubilee, and Patricia. Clearbrook had an outpost at Lake Errock. Matsqui conducted Sunday School in the village of Matsqui and constructed chapels at Silverdale and McConnell Creek. East Aldergrove built a chapel at County Line (now an independent church) and Brookswood (now South Langley MB), Arnold conducted Sunday School at Straiton.

Since the war had generated suspicion of German-speaking people, the early outreach used a non-denominational approach. However, as Mennonite Brethren took their place in the evangelical community, new

Abbotsford/McCallum Road MB Church

churches often chose names like "Community Church" or "Christian Fellowship," with MB affiliation in small print.

During the 1950's, most of the MB churches changed from a multiple ministry to a fully-salaried pastor, and worked on the language transition. Bakerview MB was begun in 1965 as a predominantly English congregation, with large contingents of members from South Abbotsford and Clearbrook. A year later, when German language services were eliminated at South Abbotsford, a group of 54 members began the German-language King Road church. During the late 1960's and 1970's many German-speaking immigrants from South America, predominantly Paraguay and Brazil, as well as USSR, gravitated to that congregation.

In 1975, at the request of Bakerview MB, the BOCE planted the Neighbourhood Bible Fellowship, later renamed Highland Community Church. Five years later, in 1980, Northview Community Church, with 64 members, was begun in rapidly expanding north-east Clearbrook. The Abbotsford Christian Fellowship began in 1986, West Clearbrook in 1989 and Mountain Park in 1991. The ethnic Mennonite Brethren in this area include the Bakerview Hispanic (1987), Indo–Canadian (1988), Abbotsford Chinese Christian (1990) and Clearbrook Vietnamese (1991). King Road began conducting Russian language services to reach recent immigrants (1992).

All the MB churches in this area belong to the B.C. Conference of Mennonite Brethren Churches. During the 1940's and 1950's, an arm of the conference, the "West Coast Children's Mission" became the catalyst for vacation Bible schools and Sunday schools in outlying areas. The WCCM was succeeded by the MB Board of Home Missions, now known as the Board of Church Extension (BOCE). During the last two decades BOCE has prompted the conference to plant ethnic as well as urban churches. This board as well as the MB conference offices are located at 202 – 2464 Clearbrook Road. The MB's founded Tabor Home in Clearbrook, and along with other Mennonite denominations, support the various endeavors of MCC.

Descendants of the immigrant farmers of the 1930's and 1940's have become acculturated business and professional people. The Mennonite Brethren have become a respected, growing evangelical denomination.

They seek to share the good news of God's gracious love and forgiveness with people of various colours, races and creed. Mennonite Brethren believe in God the Father, Jesus Christ the eternal Son of God and the Holy Spirit, one with the Father and the Son. We accept the Scriptures, and especially the teachings of Jesus, as the final biblical authority in matters of faith and life. The decision to follow Christ means committed discipleship: obedience to the Lord in all of life. The church is understood to be a body of believers, bound together in a covenant relationship based on voluntary, meaningful membership. We exercise redemptive discipline to win back those who have wandered from the path of Jesus. Our community leads to mutual concern for one another's physical and spiritual condition. We understand the Sermon on the Mount to teach a radical discipleship that must express itself in suffering love and standing for peace. The love of Christ compels every Christian to obey the Great Commission and become involved in borderless mission, uninhibited by racial or cultural boundaries.

GROWTH OF MENNONITE BRETHREN CHURCHES 1932–1992
Date of organization, church, membership figure (1992)

1930	1940	1950	1960	1970	1980	1990	2000	Membership (1992)
•1932 SA								410
•1936 NA/C								500
•1943 Arn								59
•1945–75 Mats								
•1947 EAld								429
•1950 CH								942
		•1965 BV						696
		•1966 KR						479
		•1975 HL						38
			•1980 NV					772
			•1986 ACF					16
			•1987 BVH					18
			•1988 IC					15
			•1989 WC					80
			•1990 ACCC					23
			•1991 CV					30
			•1991 MP					201

A/CH	Abbotsford/Central Heights	IC	Indo-Canadian
ACCC	Abbotsford Chinese Christian Church	KR	King Road
ACF	Abbotsford Christian Fellowship	Mats	Matsqui
Arn	Arnold	MP	Mountain Park
BV	Bakerview	NA/C	NorthAbbotsford/Clearbrook
BVH	Bakerview Hispanic	NV	Northview
CV	Clearbrook Vietnamese	SA	South Abbotsford
EAld	East Aldergrove	WC	West Clearbrook
HL	Highland		

23. Abbotsford Chinese Christian Church

In Fall, 1989, several Chinese Christian families looked in vain for a Chinese church where they might worship and serve the Lord in the Abbotsford area. They enjoyed fellowship in Vancouver on Sundays, but soon discovered that Christian fellowship on weekdays was a very important part of church life. However, driving that distance proved too stressful on the long run. They found themselves in a crisis: they needed a spiritual home. In Chinese, "crisis" is a synonym for "opportunity," so they prayed for God's guidance.

On January 4, 1990, they met in a home for Bible study. As they fellowshipped every Sunday, they prayed about the possibility of having their own church in this area. A vision developed for a new Chinese church that would be 1) a spiritual home where they could serve God, 2) a place to provide spiritual nurture for their children, and 3) a community church that would make Christ known to Chinese people in the Abbotsford area.

Persons from the core group met with Jake Balzer, chairman of the MB Board of Church Extension, and shared their vision. They firmly believed Phil. 4:19, "My God shall supply all your needs according to His riches in glory in Christ Jesus."

Soon Br. Balzer shared the exciting news that the B.C. Mennonite Brethren Conference would support the new ministry with a full-time pastor. Even more miraculous, the chapel of the King Road MB Church, a prime location, became available to them. On April 1, 1990, they conducted their first Sunday morning worship service at this location, with twelve persons attending.

A year later, the church continued to be subsidized, but aimed for a fifty percent increase in giving during the next fiscal year. They assumed responsibility for teaching their own primary Sunday School class.

On May 19, 1991, the group served a Sunday evening dinner to the King Road congregation and reported:

Pastor Yiu Tong & Elaine Chan with Dorothy & Gloria

Congregation in front of King Road chapel, 32068 King Road

"Our hearts are filled with praise and thanksgiving. Our new church has become a spiritual home for six Christian families. Many other Christians and non-Christian families find comfort and encouragement here. Five new believers have experienced conversion and two were baptized. On Friday evenings, the Abbotsford Chinese Christian Church teaches the Chinese language as a service to the local Chinese community. Attendance has grown from twelve on the first Sunday to thirty-five or more regular worshippers.

It would not be possible to realize our vision for this new church without a strong supporting church like King Road MB. May God open more doors for both of our churches to serve Him and our fellow man."

Pastor Chan directs the choir

24. Abbotsford Christian Fellowship

During the 1960's to 1980's, an increased emphasis on the work and gifts of the Holy Spirit in the life of the believer and the believer's church emerged in Christian circles. Some members of Mennonite Brethren churches in the Fraser Valley responded positively to this teaching and experienced a submission to the Holy Spirit. Their lives were and continue to be deeply affected.

A common denominator among those affected by both movements was a desire to praise and worship God using physical expressions such as clapping, raising of hands, dancing and kneeling. It was also important to allow the operation of spiritual gifts as found in 1 Cor. 12–14 both during Sunday worship services and in house fellowships.

Sunday morning worship service

Thus, a group of likeminded individuals began to meet in a home to discuss the possibility of starting an MB church where this freedom and joy could be expressed. After much prayer, regular services began in September 1986 at Terry Fox Elementary School. Abbotsford Christian Fellowship was chartered in November of that year with thirty-three members and Rev. Jake Friesen as pastor. The vision statement was taken from Isa. 61:1–3. The congregation continues to emphasize reaching out to the community as well as to the peoples of other countries with the love of Jesus.

Eventually, the congregation changed location to Abbotsford Christian Elementary School on the Mission Highway. During the past year, the congregation has experienced a variety of changes and difficul-

Left to right: Herb Klassen, Marlayne Campbell, Fred Campbell, Hart Friesen, Rev. Jake Friesen

Baptism at Matsqui Pool

ties. As of February 1992, a group of 40–50 participants continues to meet on the school premises. The emphasis on praise, worship, prayer and teaching is continuing. Sunday morning services begin with Sunday School from 9:30 to 10:15. After a break, the praise, worship and teaching service is from 10:30 to 12:00 noon. The Sunday evening prayer services are held at the church office located at Ste. 101, 32885 Ventura Ave. House fellowship groups meet on Wednesday evenings at several members' homes.

Congregation meeting at Abbotsford Christian Elementary School, summer 1991

25. Arnold Community Church

A large plot of land situated between Vedder Mountain, B.C. Hydro Rail and the Arnold slough has become known as the Arnold community. John Joseph Perrigo owned a portion of this land, but being more of a businessman than farmer, he decided to subdivide and sell to the Mennonites, somewhat similar to the model of Yarrow, B.C. Two, four and ten-acre parcels were created and listed at reasonable prices. Families coming from the prairie provinces and Vancouver Island quickly bought these plots. Berries, chickens and small herds of dairy cattle became part of the rural scene.

By 1942 eight Mennonite families had made this area their home. Mr. Perrigo offered to donate a half acre of land as a church site, provided his name would be included. The members later voted to purchase a larger parcel and use an existing name.

Arnold Mennonite Brethren Church, early 1940's

At first the German language was used in the worship services and the church was affiliated with the Yarrow Mennonite Brethren Church. Wartime restrictions on building materials prevented completion of the structure. A temporary roof was built over the basement, making it serviceable for a time. As soon as restrictions were lifted after the war, the building was completed, though by now, the growing congregation made it necessary to double the size of the original plan.

Many of the early settlers had large families. With over 200 baptized members at its zenith, church attendance sometimes went over 400. The group was blessed with a number of ordained ministers, who were chosen as the spiritual leaders. Brothers Isaac Toews, Isaac Goertzen, John B. Braun and Gustav Ratzlaff provided strong early leadership.

The change from an all-German to a bilingual German–English, and then to an all-English service did not come quickly or easily. After the war, many new immigrants who did not know the English well, arrived and slowed the transition.

In the late 1960's, a number of the pioneer settlers moved to Clearbrook to retire. With the change in language, the church attracted

some people from the community who did not have the ethnic Mennonite background.

Today members of the Arnold Community Church feel they have a unique ministry *in* the community as well as *to* the community. They realize they cannot compete with programs of the larger churches, but are able to conduct a closer knit program. They strive to be a friendly church that ministers to the needs of local families.

Completed church, late 1940's

Arnold Community Church today

26. BAKERVIEW MENNONITE BRETHREN CHURCH

THE PAST

The Bakerview Church had its origins in the Clearbrook MB Church, which was filled to capacity during the 1960's, as more and more people moved into the area. In addition the church faced a growing desire among some members for a more rapid change in language and worship styles. Early in 1965 people who wished to organize a new church were invited to put their names on a confidential list.

An organizational meeting was held on March 15, 1965. After a communion service with the mother church, which contributed financially toward the construction of a place of worship, the new congregation met separately for the first time on April 11, 1965 at Columbia Bible College. By this time, one of the original sig-nators of the list of intent, Br. H. Lenzmann, the only senior citizen in the group, had passed away.

Original Bakerview MB Church

During its first ten years, the church grew from 103 original members to 430. An expansion of the educational facilities was undertaken during the mid 1970's, but this did not solve the problem of overcrowding in the Sunday worship services. Dual services began in September, 1977. Additional lots adjacent to the church were purchased for future expansion. In 1986 a major renovation and expansion project enlarged the foyer and added a gym and second floor to the education wing.

THE PRESENT

Both the programs and composition of the Bakerview Church have changed during its brief history. The church is home to three distinct congregations. The largest, consisting of 700 members, conducts two Sunday services in English. Its growth includes new families moving into the area and seniors retiring here. A growing Spanish-speaking church also meets in the building. It helps refugees coming to Canada and set-tling in this area. A Vietnamese congregation meeting at Bakerview min-isters to immigrants from South East Asia. To assist the newcomers, an English as a Second Language program is offered by Bakerview Church.

Expanded Bakerview facilities, 2285 Clearbrook Road

In its strong music pro-
gram, Bakerview provides a
balance of traditional and
contemporary music.
Besides the chancel choir,
the church has a choir for
seniors and one for children.
Programs in recreation,
travel and service have been
designed for the growing
seniors group. In 1991 the
church launched a new
Logos Program for chil-

Children's ministry at Bakerview

dren. Instead of dividing families, it involves the whole family in food,
fellowship and other activities once a week. The Bakerview Church provides Christian education for all ages. This includes College/Career and
an active youth program.

THE FUTURE

The Bakerview Church presently has a pastoral staff of six, and additional staff for the Spanish and Vietnamese congregations. If growth patterns continue, extra
staff will likely be
added and creative use
of facilities imple-
mented. Additional
property has been
purchased for possible
future expansion.

Peter Enns

"Kids' Recreation," part of Bakerview's community service.

27. Bakerview Hispanic Mennonite Brethren Church

The Bakerview Hispanic congregation traces its beginnings to the early spring of 1987. A growing number of refugees from El Salvador, Honduras and Nicaragua began settling in the Clearbrook–Abbotsford area. Through the outreach efforts of the Bakerview Mennonite Brethren Church, a small group began meeting informally for Bible Study and prayer.

Frank & Sally Schroeder Isaak

On October 5, 1987, Sally Schroeder Isaak, a retired missionary from Ecuador, began a Spanish Sunday school class at Bakerview. Five Latin Americans attended the first class, 13 the next Sunday. Although the participating "Latinos" came from different countries, belonged to different churches and held opposing political views, the group began to jell. By Christmas attendance reached 25.

When participants asked for weekly Spanish worship services, it was decided to meet for singing, Bible Study and fellowship at the church on Wednesday nights. Women in the group took turns caring for small children.

In September, 1988, Isaac and Adaly Hernandez moved to Clearbrook and started attending services. On March 1, 1989, Isaac, an experienced pastor from El Salvador, was appointed a pastoral intern in a leadership team consisting of Isaac Hernandez, Sally Isaak and David Falk. On May 1, 1990, he became the first full-time pastor of the congregation. He served as pastor until September of 1991. Presently Sylvester Dirks, a retired missionary from Peru, serves as interim pastor. The congregation is seeking a replacement for Hernandez.

The Bakerview Hispanic Church is jointly funded by the Hispanic congregation, the Bakerview Church and the B.C. Conference of Mennonite Brethren Churches. The congregation celebrated the official charter membership service on March 2, 1991. The present adult mem-

Isaac & Adaly Hernandez, Karen and Jesse   *Syl & Mattie Dirks*

bership of the congregation stands at 21, with a regular attendance of 50–60.

The Bakerview Hispanic Mennonite Brethren Church meets in the facilities of the Bakerview Church at 2285 Clearbrook Road in Clearbrook. Weekly events include:

Worship Service	Saturday	7:30 PM
Midweek Bible Study	Wednesday	7:30 PM
Prayer Meeting	Friday	7:30 PM
Youth Fellowship	Friday	7:30 PM

More information regarding the Bakerview Hispanic congregation can be obtained by contacting the church by telephone (859-4611).

28. CENTRAL HEIGHTS MENNONITE BRETHREN CHURCH
A Place For You

There's a place for you at Central Heights Church. Since 1950 the Central Heights family has been reaching out in love to our community.

Senior Pastor Pete Unrau

Our purpose is to meet your spiritual needs in a warm fellowship of love and acceptance where genuine long-term friendships are formed.

The pulpit ministry is dedicated to Bible-centered preaching that has relevance to your daily life.

Come and join us! Our doors and our hearts are open to you, our neighbours. We look forward to meeting you and developing new friendships.

ADULT MINISTRY: A full range of adult home fellowship groups meet weekly. Adult groups meet each Sunday during the family Bible Hour for Bible instruction.

MUSIC & WORSHIP: Music is an integral part of congregational worship. There are many ways you can participate as a vocalist or instrumentalist.

MISSIONS & EVANGELISM: Preparing and sending out missionaries is both our privilege and duty. We are blessed with a large number of full-time and part-time missionaries serving around the world.

YOUTH MINISTRY: The youth ministry complements your family

Opportunities abound for vocalists and instrumentalists in our active music ministries

We worship to honour and discover the excellencies of God.

by helping to meet the complex needs of Junior and Senior High young people.

WOMEN'S MINISTRY: Programs such as "Time Out," "Open Door Fellowship," and "Prayer for Power" are committed to reaching out to the community, to missionaries, to prisoner's spouses, and to handicapped. Come and be encouraged.

YOUNG ADULT MINISTRY: The young adults meet regularly for fun, fellowship, and study of God's Word. We attempt to help you meet the unique new challenges you face as a young adult.

Children's ministries include Sunday School classes, midweek clubs, and the unique Caravan St. program

SENIORS' MINISTRY: Seniors are special people. A variety of Bible classes, missions, recreational activities, and "New Horizons" groups are geared to meet the needs of seniors.

CHILDREN'S MINISTRY: A variety of programs, both Sundays and midweek, are designed to meet the special needs of your children. We also offer a licensed Preschool for 3 to 4 year olds.

SUNDAY WORSHIP SCHEDULE:

    8:30 & 11:00 AM Morning Worship
    9:50 AM   Sunday School Hour
    6:30 PM   Celebration Service

Everyone is welcome!

29. Clearbrook Mennonite Brethren Church

Clearbrook MB Church began on January 24, 1936 with a group that met in homes, first at the Gerhard Rempel's and then at the William Wiebe's. Rempel was elected as leader. The congregation, called North Abbotsford MB Church, purchased a plot of land on the corner of Old Yale and Clearbrook roads and built its first church. The present church building was constructed in 1957 and remodelled in 1991.

Clearbrook Mennonite Brethren Church, 2719 Clearbrook Road

A love for and faith in God's Word has characterized and shaped the development of the church. The preaching of the Word of God has always been a very important part of regular Sunday services. Mid-week Bible studies and prayer meetings, as well as Bible conferences, have contributed to its spiritual growth and vitality.

The church identifies with the MB Conference in doctrine and practice, as well as supporting provincial, Canadian and General Conference projects. It contributes financially to the MB missions and many faith missions, as well as MCC .

Many missionaries who have gone abroad or served in our own country, have roots in Clearbrook MB Church. Several churches, East Aldergrove MB and Bakerview MB were started by members of Clearbrook. In 1960, a mission church was built at Lake Errock and members of Clearbrook MB served that congregation for some time.

The growth and development of the church was determined by a number of factors, including its location and bilingual (German &

English) services. The majority of new members have been senior citizens who have retired in adult-oriented condos near the church. With backgrounds in Europe and German-speaking areas, many of them preferred the German language.

Although the church had a small beginning, the membership stood at 738 in 1964. Ten years later it was 720. As of January 1, 1992 the membership was 516, predominantly senior citizens. Sunday services are held in two languages—German and English. The German service begins at 9:50 AM and the English service at 11:00 AM. The evening services are usually in English, thus ministering to people in the community. Everyone is welcome.

Bible studies are conducted on Wednesday evenings in both languages, with the groups meeting in separate rooms. Sunday School and youth classes, though small, are provided as needed. Other ministries to children includes a weekly AWANA Club program on Tuesdays after school and Vacation Bible School classes in the summer.

Four separate ladies' groups meet for fellowship and ministry. Much of their work is channelled through MCC. A large number of men and women from the church work on a voluntary, part-time basis at the MCC Plaza, thus contributing substantially to world relief. Many other facets in the ministry of the church have not been listed here.

The leadership team at Clearbrook MB Church consists of Jacob & Mary Pauls, John & Leona Klassen, George and Mary Baier (music ministries) and Heather Wiebe (office secretary).

Jacob & Mary Pauls

John & Leona Klassen

30. Clearbrook Vietnamese Mennonite Brethren Church

The first Vietnamese refugees settled in the Clearbrook–Abbotsford area in 1979. Many of these were sponsored by Fraser Valley churches. Presently this area is home to 800–1000 Vietnamese immigrants.

Pastor Cam Loc Le, a Vancouver Vietnamese pastor, began meeting with a group in Clearbrook in 1985, assisted by two Vietnamese students at Columbia Bible College. Ken Ha and Timothy Ma, sensed the need for a more permanent church in this area, and in 1987 Ken became the part-time pastor of the congregation. With the financial assistance of the Bakerview Church and the Mennonite Brethren Board of Church Extension, he was appointed full-time pastor in 1988 and continues to serve this congregation.

The Clearbrook Vietnamese Mennonite Brethren Church is jointly funded by the Vietnamese congregation, the Bakerview Church and the B.C. Conference of Mennonite Brethren Churches. On November 3, 1991 the Vietnamese Church held its charter membership service. Currently it has an adult membership of 18, with an average attendance of 37.

Ken & Ruth Ha, with Joseph, Daniel and Elizabeth

Charter Members

The Clearbrook Vietnamese Mennonite Brethren Church meets in the facilities of the Bakerview Church at 2285 Clearbrook Road. Weekly services include:

Worship Service   Sunday   3:00 PM
Prayer Meeting   Wednesday   7:30 PM
Youth Fellowship   Friday   7:30 PM

For more information call 852-9690 or 859-6319.

Baptismal Service

31. EAST ALDERGROVE MENNONITE BRETHREN CHURCH

The East Aldergrove MB Church was begun in 1947 by 32 families, members of North Abbotsford Church, living in the Aldergrove area.

They bought five acres of land on the corner of Ross and Maclure Roads. Only the basement was built the first year. On June 15 the church was officially organized with about 80 members and named East Aldergrove MB church. The first pastor was Rev. Gerhard Warkentin, a dairy farmer.

The Lord chose to work in our humble basement. Many commitments were made. Baptisms and celebrations as well as funerals and weddings were held. The building was completed in spring 1949 and dedicated on April 18.

East Aldergrove sent missionaries to several foreign countries. Others served in the homeland in church planting, teaching among the natives, and conducting Sunday school in more remote areas. These efforts helped to build two other churches: Countyline and South Langley.

When Rev. Warkentin resigned in 1956, Rev. Herman Voth became our pastor. The transition from the German to the English language occurred during the Voth's eight-year ministry.

Rev. C.D. Toews became the next pastor. During this time Pioneer Girls and Boys Brigade clubs were started.

Rudie Willms from Winnipeg assumed pastoral duties in August 1970. When the church grew, Jake Martens and Wilf Richert served as part-time assistants. An educational wing was built and after a few years, a multi-purpose section including a gym and kitchen was added. In 1980 Neil and Elizabeth Klassen became the first full-time associate pastor couple. In 1981, when the building became overcrowded, a new sanctuary was built on the same site as the old one. The Willms served for 14 years.

When both couples left, Dan Warkentin served as youth and interim pastor until Rev. John Froese came and served as pastor for 4 years. He was followed by Rev. Jay Neufeld in 1988.

Original East Aldergrove Church with educational wing

Our purpose is to

unitedly ascribe glory to God by our praise, worship, and daily walk, by being a caring community of growing disciples who study God's Word and are led by the Holy Spirit, and by loving the lost as we share the Lord Jesus with them and accept them into our fellowship.

Membership class with Pastor Neufeld and Paetkau

Our current staff includes Jay Neufeld — senior pastor, Will Born — youth minister, Jerrold Paetkau — Christian Education director, Arnold & Ruth Klassen — music ministers. Our church family includes over 400 people. Many volunteers work in their areas of interest, giftedness, or obvious talent. Facilities are currently being expanded.

Our church programs include Sunday school, deacon ministry hospital and home visitation, mid-week Care Group Bible study and prayer in homes, Pioneer boys/girls on Wednesday evenings, Open Door ministry for single moms, youth ministry: Bible studies and social activities, and ladies clubs that sew materials for needy countries. Baptism and membership classes are offered regularly.

Our church family is warm and friendly. If you are looking for a church home, come and join us. We have room for you. The East Aldergrove Church at 3160 Ross Road begins the first Sunday service at 8:45 AM, Sunday School at 10:00 AM and the second service at 11:10 AM.

East Aldergrove Mennonite Brethren Church Family

32. Highland Community Church
"A Place for Reconnecting"

During the early 1970's the church at large was struggling to come to terms with the youth counter-culture and the spiritual renewal which accompanied it. The MB churches of the Matsqui–Abbotsford area responded by envisioning the birth of a congregation which would capture the ideals, values and renewed energy of this movement. Facilitated by Nick Dyck, then director of the Board of Church Extension. A call was extended to persons interested in forming a new congregation. It became a rallying point for those looking for A NEW WAY TO BE CONNECTED to the life of the church.

The group, calling themselves the Neighborhood Bible Fellowship, began meeting in fall 1975, in the chapel of Columbia Bible Institute. The vision which emerged during the first year included renewed worship, organizing around family life, relating significantly to the community at large and plural leadership.

Kirk Digitale began his nine-year ministry with the congregation in the fall of 1976. He established solid Biblical instruction as one of the congregation's distinguishing marks. In 1980, with the aid of a donation of land by a generous individual in the Conference and substantial monetary gifts from sister churches, the congregation constructed its own building and was renamed Highland Community Church.

The church operated for four years in the mid-80's with either unpaid or partially-supported leaders, Elmer Dyck and Dan Stobbe. In fall 1988, Roland Balzer began ministering as full-time pastoral elder.

Over the years Highland Community Church has been a place where

Highland Community Church, 3130 McMillan Road

persons who have become disenchanted
with their religious experience or otherwise
distanced from the church have been able to
GENTLY RE-CONNECT with God their Father
and His people, the church.

RE-CONNECT TO THE LIVING GOD —
We believe that nurturing a dynamic rela-
tionship with the living God is the most important aspect of our personal
and corporate life. We invite others to accept and grow in that relationship through intentionally becoming accountable to another individual
and to a small care and study group for spiritual growth, through accepting thoughtful teaching on Sundays and in small groups during the week,
and through worship which gives prayerful attention to the living presence of the Spirit of both the Father and the Son.

RE-CONNECT WITH PERSONS, ACCEPTING THEM AS UNIQUELY
WORTHWHILE AND CARING FOR THEM — We believe that the church is
a place of belonging for families and singles. We invite others to participate in small care and study groups, in Ladies Time Out, in youth group,
in children's activity nights and in women's and men's prayer groups.

RE-CONNECT WITH GOD'S WORK IN THE WORLD — We believe that
we are called to cooperate in God's mission of bringing all things back
into harmony with Himself and we invite others to become God's agents
with us. This occurs in our corporate ministry to the
Matsqui–Abbotsford community: the Columbia Christian Counselling
Group and Ladies Time Out. It happens though affirming each other's
ministries in the community through word and deed, as well as our support of agencies such as MCC and MB Missions/Services.

As a RE-CONNECTING PLACE, Highland Community Church is a
community of people who know that they are loved by God and are
learning to love Him and others:
through celebration and service
under the Lordship of Jesus Christ
empowered by the Holy Spirit.

33. KING ROAD MENNONITE BRETHREN CHURCH

The King Road MB Church celebrated its 25th anniversary in October, 1991. In the mid 1960's, when a number of MB churches discontinued bilingual English–German services, a number of people wished to continue worship in the German language. Some 54 persons, largely from the South Abbotsford MB Church, became charter members in October, 1966. They met in the vacant Poplar United Church at the corner of King and Clearbrook Roads and purchased the property in 1967. A new building was erected and dedicated on October 15 of that year. The congregation grew, necessitating an addition and educational wing in 1976.

King Road Church, 1967

A large modern sanctuary and gymnasium/fellowship hall, completed in 1983, now provides ample room for the present congregation of some 450 members and children. People who are Canadian-born, as well as immigrants from Europe and South America have found a church home here. The pastors of this congregation have been Jacob P. Dueck (1966–70), Jacob H. Franz (1971–78), Peter C. Penner (1978–81), A. J. Klassen (1981–85), and Abe J. Konrad (1986–). Rufus Loewen (1983–88) and Hermann Stahl (1989–) have served in youth ministries and Ben Pauls (1992–) in worship and music.

Since April 1991, Sunday morning worship services in German are conducted at 9:50, while the English worship service begins at 11:00. Both services feature congregational singing, special music by choirs or groups and the preaching of God's Word.

Sunday School classes for both children and adults are conducted in English as well as German. Other ministries include mid-week programs for young children, Pioneer Girls and Christian Service Brigade, youth groups, College and Career as well as mid-week Bible study and small group adult Bible studies in homes.

Music at King Road satisfies a variety of tastes: traditional hymns as well as modern Scripture songs and choruses.

The King Road Church has strong interest in mission. A number of members have and are serving abroad. The church supports individual missionaries as well as the denominational Board of Missions/ Services and serves as home base for the German radio broadcast "Message of Peace." Ministries of compassion are supported in practical

Thanksgiving celebration

ways through the MCC. The Abbotsford Chinese Christian Church meets in the old chapel.

The purpose of the King Road MB Church is to proclaim the message of Jesus Christ for the salvation of immortal souls, to strengthen and nurture believers through the Word of God under the guidance of the Holy Spirit and to minister to the needs of people in such a way that the compassion and love of Christ is practically experienced.

King Road MB Church has the unique opportunity of ministering in two languages, English and German, thus building bridges of understanding between generations and cultures as people come from South America and Europe to make their home in the Fraser Valley. To this calling we want to be true, encouraging our members to use their spiritual gifts in the work of the church for the honour and glory of God.

King Road MB Church, 32068 King Road, 1983

34. MOUNTAIN PARK COMMUNITY CHURCH
"Exalting Christ and Encouraging One Another"

Christ establishes churches to be His "body" in a world of growing need. So that we will not forget and coming generations will remember what the Lord has done, we recount the beginnings of Mountain Park Community Church.

BEGINNING WITH A VISION
Mountain Park Community Church began with the vision of the BOCE of the BC Conference of MB Churches, to establish a church in East Abbotsford. Interested persons met to pray regarding the organization of this new church and the involvement of Pastor Herbert & Adeline Neufeld as the senior pastor couple. At a subsequent meeting it was agreed to invite Pastor Walter & Shirley Janzen to join the pastoral staff and to trust the Lord for the necessary finances.

With the support of the BOCE the first "Interest Meeting" was held on April 29, 1991 at the Nazarene Church on McMillan Road. Approximately 140 adults attended. A growing number of families committed themselves to being part of this new church.

Young couples enjoy "Christmas at the Farm, '91"

God confirmed His direction for the church through financial provision as well as the donation of equipment including a furniture van to transport chairs, a 44 passenger bus and office space.

STEERING COMMITTEE
The first steering committee consisted of men and women who shared the vision, planned and hosted events and supported the pastoral team.

FIRST PUBLIC WORSHIP SERVICE, SEPTEMBER 8, 1991
The Abbotsford School Board made it possible to rent the gymnasium and several classrooms at Yale Secondary School. In faith, approximately

200 chairs were set up in anticipation of the first group of worshippers. What a joy it was to scramble to set up an additional 175 chairs on September 8! In subsequent weeks, the average attendance stabilized at approximately 375. Soon Dave Heinrichs joined the staff as part-time Youth Intern.

MEMBERSHIP SUNDAY, DECEMBER 8, 1991

On December 8, 164 individuals expressed their commitment to Mountain Park by officially becoming members. The first baptism class soon began and eight believers were baptized at McMillan Pool on December 29, 1991 to bring the membership to 172.

FURTHER DEVELOPMENTS

The Board of Elders recently signed an option to purchase a 7.44 acre site in the East Abbotsford area for a permanent church home.

We welcome all to join us for our worship services at Yale Secondary School on Sundays at 10:30 a.m. Services include both traditional and contemporary expressions: drama, special music, and personal faith stories.

Mutual care and love are expressed in "Care Groups" which meet in homes, providing a relaxed setting for 'newcomers.'

It is our desire to exalt Christ and to encourage one another. "Now to Him who is able to do immeasurably more than all we ask or imagine, according to His power that is at work within us, to Him be glory in the church and in Christ Jesus throughout all generations, for ever and ever! Amen." (Ephesians 3:20–21 NIV)

Teresa J Klassen

Baptism at McMillan Pool. Pastor Herb
Neufeld and Brenda Arnau

First group of baptized members

35. Northview Community Church

From 1981 to 1986 the Abbotsford–Matsqui district was Canada's fastest growing area with a population increase of 16.58 per cent. Due to the foresight of evangelically-minded individuals, Northview's founding was strategically timed to reach out to this growing population.

Early in 1980, several pastors met with Nick Dyck requesting that the BOCE of the MB Conference consider starting a new church in this area. With the encouragement of the MB pastors and approval of the board, interested people met at the Columbia Bible Institute chapel on March 27, 1980. The name, Northview Community Church reflects Northview's highly community-oriented emphasis.

MB families and individuals from the Central Heights, Bakerview, and South Abbotsford became involved in the formation of Northview. The first formal meeting was held September 7, 1980 at the new MEI facilities.

On November 23, 1980, 58 persons signed as charter members. The first pastoral couple, Merv and Carol Boschman, served from May, 1981 through Spring 1987. The congregation reached an average attendance of 430 by July, 1988.

In August, 1988 the church occupied its new facilities at 32040 Downes Road. This, together with the call of Pastor Vern and Carol Heidebrecht to lead the ministry team, promoted growth. Today the four worship services average over 1,600 in total attendance.

Pastor Frank Martens leads a team of over 50 home Care Groups to strengthen integration and care-giving. The Learning Center and children's ministries are led by Pastor Dwayne Koop. Marj Wiebe serves as pastor of discipleship and leads new life classes, women's and men's ministries.

Family and Youth ministries are headed by Pastor Dave Currie and several associates. Northview is a worship center with a dynamic contemporary music ministry led by Pastor Wayne Loewen in a refreshing praise and worship style.

Pastor Vern and Carol Heidebrecht

Northview Community Church, 32040 Downes Road

The committed team of elders provides leadership for the congregation and the staff. "The goal is to move people from spectator to participant in the work of the church and the community," states moderator Don Voth.

Jesus Christ is the center·of Northview. Our purpose statement glorifies Him and sets our direction:

UPWARD: GOD-CENTERED
           Celebrating God's presence through praise, worship and
           prayer
INWARD: PEOPLE-FRIENDLY
           Encouraging and preparing people for life and service
           through Scriptural instruction, training and fellowship
OUTWARD: WORLD-FOCUSED
           Reaching out to Abbotsford, Canada and the World
           with the Good News of Jesus Christ through the
           enabling of the Holy Spirit.

In March, 1992 an additional ten acres east of the original ten-acre property were purchased. Enlarging the facilities will make room for the growing congregation.

Vision to serve has led to partnering with Christians in Mexico City in church planting, summer projects among the native people in the North and focus on target ministries in our community.

Since the founding of the congregation our goal has been that we be equipped through gathering for worship and instruction in order to evangelize as we scatter into our homes and marketplace.

36. South Abbotsford Mennonite Brethren Church

The South Abbotsford MB Church was the first Mennonite Brethren Church to be established in the Matsqui–Abbotsford area. Its origins go back to 1931, when this area was being opened up for settlement. The church began on May 1, 1932 as the Abbotsford MB Church and met in the Farmers Institute Hall under the auspices of the Yarrow MB Church. It conducted the first baptism on July 10, 1932. Since the church had grown considerably by Fall, 1935, it was divided into two congregations: North Abbotsford MB Church and South Abbotsford MB Church.

The church, with a membership of 137, purchased land on the corner of Gladwin and Huntington Roads and constructed its first sanctuary for the total sum of $811.24! Continual growth led to the construction of a new church on its present site on the corner of Huntington and Columbia Roads, dedicated on July 27, 1953. Since then the church has undertaken several expansions and is currently planning another addition and renovation to meet its expanding needs and programs.

Throughout its history, the South Abbotsford MB church has promoted Christian education among young people. It established the MB Bible School (now CBC), in 1943) and the MEI in 1944. Spreading the Gospel locally was accomplished through travelling music groups, home Bible studies, mission Sunday Schools, Vacation Bible Schools, and establishing new churches such as the McCallum Road Church (now Central Heights).

South Abbotsford MB Church, 32424 Huntington Road

During its sixty years of existence, the South Abbotsford MB Church has not lost its purpose and vision. A team of five pastors: Cliff Janzen, senior pastor; David Epp, personal ministries; Ed Balzer, music and Christian Education; David Manuel, Indo–Canadian ministries; and Randy Thompson, youth ministries, serves its 400 members and the surrounding community. As it was in 1932, so it is still the major purpose of the church to offer reverent and humble worship to God. Through its Christian education program, it assists its adherents in becoming mature, witnessing disciples, living righteously according to God's Word, the Bible. And by it programs and projects, it shares the Good News locally, nationally, and internationally.

David & Stella Manuel

A major thrust of the South Abbotsford MB Church has been to bring the Gospel to the Indo–Canadian community in the Matsqui–Abbotsford area. Since 1980 David and Stella Manuel have been working among their people, so that now a group of Indo–Canadians meets here every Sunday for worship and fellowship. Once a membership of 15 or more is established, the group hopes to charter as an independent MB congregation.

In addition to local ministries, South Abbotsford supports some twenty different missionaries directly, as well as international ministries through the Mennonite Brethren Board of Missions and Services, and the Mennonite Central Committee.

Fellowship at the 11th Annual Bible Conference, 1991

Pastor Cliff Janzen states that many churches, after sixty years, have ceased to exist. But by God's grace, the South Abbotsford MB Church continues to exist as a vibrant and energetic part of the Church of Jesus Christ.

Wally Sawatzky

Ministries to old and young

37. West Clearbrook Community Church

West Clearbrook Community Church was established by the MB BOCE because existing facilities were overcrowded and community growth made another church viable, particularly in the west Clearbrook area. In order to establish the level of interest in a new church, several meetings were held in spring 1989. Subsequently, the BOCE hired Bert Kamphuis as pastor and set up a temporary steering.

The church began holding Sunday morning services in the CBC chapel in September 1989. October 29, 1989 was its charter membership Sunday and in June 1990 the group officially joined the MB Conference of B.C.

In 1991 the congregation developed a purpose statement which reads: The purpose of our church is to bring peace to our families and community as well as the world through our commitment to Jesus Christ. This purpose is achieved through providing opportunities for fellowship, worship, teaching, service and sharing Christian hope.

In the church's short history this has included a number of involvements. In addition to the usual Sunday activities there are midweek care and study

Sunday morning worship service

Congregation with 36 charter members

groups. An after school Kids' Club meets at CBC. A number of people are involved in the M2 and prison fellowship programs. Others assist in the Open Door child care program at the Emmanuel Mennonite Church. Members of the congregation participate in various missionary ventures. Some members

Baptism, 1989 l.–r. Aaron Vooys, Eric Janzen, Mark Steinbach

work for the MCC supportive care services. Others volunteer in various community organizations.

The church hopes to continue promoting the peaceful community well-being that characterizes right relationships between people and God, between individuals, and between people and creation through its various ministries.

Linda Matties

Commissioning of first missionary, Rob Dyck

Congregation of West Clearbrook Community Church, pastor Bert Kamphuis, front left

38. The Free Methodist Church

OUR PAST

The Free Methodist Church in this area began in September 1983, with Rev. Joe James as the founding pastor. The first public worship service was held at the Abbotsford Senior High School. Shortly after that their services were moved to the Seventh Day Adventist Church on Griffiths Street where the church continues to meet.

OUR PRESENT

Pastoral Leadership

Pastor Cam Taylor, Vicky, Caleb & Elena

Sunday Worship and Sunday School
9:45 a.m.   Sunday School
                Nursery to Young Teen plus Adult classes
11:00 a.m.   Worship Service
                Nursery & children's church provided

CARE GROUPS AND FELLOWSHIP TIMES

Care Groups meet for Bible Study, sharing and prayer

Ministry to children is an important part of our program

Informal get-togethers help build friendships

WE ARE A CHURCH...

Small Enough...

    where you are known by name

    where you find meaning and significance

    where one person can make a difference

But Big Enough...

    to have programs for children, young teens, and adults

    to have care groups for your support and encouragement

    to have a worship style that is balanced between old and new

OUR PURPOSE

"To worship God, prepare for ministry, build relationships and be a witness to the world."

We presently meet at 1921 Griffiths Road (a Seventh Day Adventist Church)

Church Office: 004A – 2580 Cedar Park Place, Clearbrook
Telephone: Office: 859-4774
    Residence: 859-6981

39. ABBOTSFORD CHURCH OF THE NAZARENE

Earliest beginnings of the Abbotsford Church of the Nazarene go back to 1923, when a group of local women held prayer meetings in the Presbyterian Church. Interest in the Church of the Nazarene and its doctrine of holiness was sparked by Mrs. Edith Spaulding who had read some issues of the *Herald of Holiness*, the official periodical of this young denomination which started in the U.S.A. in 1908. Then Mrs. J.T. Heppell, a member of the Cloverdale Church of the Nazarene, became acquainted with the group and introduced them to her minister, Rev. L.E. Channell. He commuted from Cloverdale to Abbotsford by B.C. Electric train to provide leadership for the meetings held in homes.

In May 1924, they rented the Orange Hall on Pauline Street, across from the present lawn bowling field. By June, a Sunday School of 26 members was organized with Mrs. Spaulding as Sunday School superintendent. Regular Sunday afternoon services were conducted by Rev. Channell.

Since the membership grew, plans to erect a church building were made in December 1924. Mr. and Mrs. John Arnold donated a lot at the corner of Essendene and Pauline Streets and construction began. Rev. James H. Bury, supervised the erection of the two-storey church with the sanctuary in the upper storey. The parsonage below doubled as Sunday School rooms.

Under the leadership of Rev. L. E. Channell, the church was organized with 15 charter members, on February 15, 1925. In 1927, the Nazarene Women's Missionary Society, with Mrs. John Arnold as president and a Nazarene Young People's Society were started. A complete church program was under way.

To accommodate the growing Sunday School, the edifice was enlarged under the leadership of both Rev. George Hartzell (1928–29)

First Church Building on Pauline Street (1924–49)

and Rev. R. E. Lawrence (1934–40). A camp meeting was held in the Orange Hall in July 1940 with record attendance.

A branch Sunday School was begun at Straiton during Rev. R. E. Lawrence and Rev. A. J. Loughton's ministry (1940–43). A well-trained choir under the direction of Rev. E. Culbertson (1945–1947) often presented seasonal musicals. During the ministry of Rev. William Baptiste (1947–50), a parsonage was purchased on Mountain View Road and new property obtained at the corner of McCallum and Cannon Roads. Soon construction on a new church was begun, but only the basement was finished. The old "landmark" church on Essendene was sold.

During the leadership of Rev. Alex B. Patterson (1951–54), the church at Cannon and McCallum Roads, together with a spacious parsonage, was completed and dedicated on November 23, 1949.

The church left its lasting mark on many lives during the pastorates of Rev. George MacDonald (1955–58), Rev. Maurice Westmacott (1958–63), Rev. Cyril Palmer (1963–67), Rev. A. J. Loughton (Supply), Rev. E. M. Culbertson (1968–73), Rev. Raymond Friberg (1974–77), Rev. Mark Caldwell (1977–80) and Rev. Donald Nicholas (1980–86).

Relocation and construction of a larger complex with adequate Sunday School rooms and a gymnasium became imperative to assure continued church growth. Property was purchased on McMillan Road and in August 1980 the church and parsonage on McCallum were sold and plans initiated to erect the present church building. Under Rev. Don Nicholas, the church was completed and dedicated on October 4, 1981. It provides fine educational, nursery and kitchen facilities, as well as a daycare centre, "The Open Door". This government-approved school offers

Second Church Building at McCallum and Cannon (1949–80)

day care, kindercare, preschool care and out-of-school care for children up to twelve years of age. A recent addition to the church is Jonah's Beach House, a youth centre built to accommodate youth of the church and from the community around Yale Secondary School. On Sunday, January 26, 1992, the Youth Centre was dedicated by our pastor, Rev. Ross Johnston (1987–) and youth minister, Barry McLeod.

The statement of purpose of this church affirms that its people are committed to:

LOVING GOD — by worship that exalts Christ, and by lives that glorify God;

LOVING EACH OTHER — through caring relationships in which serving, discipling, equipping and releasing to ministry are ongoing; and

LOVING THE WORLD — by sharing Christ, His love, His healing and His resources.

We rejoice in the privileges God has given us to do so in this wonderful community.

Present Church Facilities, 2390 McMillan Road (1981–)

40. ABBOTSFORD PENTECOSTAL ASSEMBLY

In the fall of 1926, William Kennedy, a local saw filer requested that John C. MacKenzie hold evangelistic meetings in Matsqui. After contacting Mr. MacKenzie, Kennedy rented the Orange Hall and scheduled services. Before long, Mr. MacKenzie was asked to pastor the small congregation. The church that was established became affiliated with the Pentecostal Assemblies of Canada. The Orange Hall remained its meeting place for approximately one year. However, late in 1927 the group moved to 32900 South Fraser Way, the second floor served as both church and parsonage.

In 1928, Rev. A. J. Edwards led a building program which erected a church at the corner of Montrose and Laurel, on a lot donated by the J. Caldwell family. Unfortunately, it was destroyed by a fire in 1933.

In 1934 the congregation met in the Masonic Hall and later rented 33889 Essendene Avenue.

Under the direction of Rev. Horace Robertson a new church was completed on the original site at the corner of Laurel and Montrose. In 1956, this building was sold to the Bethel Reformed Church.

Church at Laurel & Montrose

Last Sunday at 2420 Montrose

Parkview Villa

In 1957, Rev. J. V. Ruthven piloted the erection of a 400-seat church at 2420 Montrose Avenue. This building was sold and recently renovated, currently housing Abbotsford's Community Services.

On May 22, 1968 the Parkview Villa Society was incorporated by members of the Abbotsford Pentecostal Assembly. In 1970, it completed the construction of a six-story, low rental accommodation for senior citizens. This complex is located at 33433 Switzer Avenue just behind Motorcade. Currently, the Parkview Villa operates smoothly and is filled to capacity.

In 1975, Rev. Gordon Lucas led the congregation in a building project at our current site, 3145 Gladwin Road. This building remains an integral part of our present facility.

On March 12, 1989, under the leadership of Rev. Calvin C. Ratz, ground was broken for construction of our present facility. It represents the culmination of a five-year plan for expansion of the ministries and programs of the Abbotsford Pentecostal Assembly. The new 1,650 seat sanctuary is bright and beautiful. The con-

Church at 3145 Gladwin, 1976

gregation also enjoys the benefits of additional offices, Christian Education space and an expanded gymnasium.

Our church has been a place of worship to many throughout the years. Though the actual church "building" is important, the true "church" consists of many people who make up the body of Christ in Abbotsford and around the world. Our building serves as a church home for many faithful men and women of God. Yet, as we reflect on our beginnings and read a brief account of our history, we see the blessing and guidance of the hand of God.

As a congregation, we put our trust in the Lord for His continued guidance and direction in the ministry of Abbotsford Pentecostal Assembly. We pray that our church will be viewed as a place of refuge to those within our community who wish to worship with us and to those who are still seeking Him.

Dr. Paul Hawkes, Pastor

Abbotsford Pentecostal Assembly today

41. Bradner Presbyterian Church

The congregation of the Bradner Presbyterian Church dates back to the mid 1920's, when Presbyterians gathered for worship in various places throughout the area. The present church building was erected in 1932. Thus 1992 marks the 60th anniversary of the construction of this place of worship.

Bradner Presbyterian Church, 5275 Bradner Road

For many years, the Bradner congregation was part of a multiple point charge. Ministers and lay elders from Vancouver, Abbotsford or Mission served the church. Among those who took the services were Wilburt Lyle, Hamish Harvey, Rev. Murdo Pollock, Rev. Desmond Howard, Rev. Bob Calder, and Rev. Amy Campbell. During the 1980's the church experienced considerable growth under the leadership of Rev. David Webber, who served as the first full-time pastor until he was called to pioneer a new ministry in the Cariboo.

Today the church is experiencing a new challenge to grow and reach out into the community. Although there is no Sunday School at present, it may be re-established since a few new families have been attending. An active youth group has doubled from five to ten kids since its beginning in the Fall. Special events held each year include the November Bake Sale and the Irish Supper in March.

To celebrate the 60th anniversary, the former minister Rev. David Webber has been invited as guest preacher, assisted by the moderator of our Presbytery, Rev. Charles Scott, and the missions convenor, Rev. Kerry McIntyre of Chilliwack.

With the resignation of Rev. Amy Campbell in June 1991, the Presbytery appointed Dr. Cal Chambers as interim moderator. He is a retired minister, but serves the church on a part-time basis. Under his leadership, the congregation has experienced significant growth and developed a spirit of optimism regarding the future. The Session is served by four elders, with Mrs. Sarah Arnold as the clerk and Mr. Clint Dunningtom as chairperson of the board of managers. The church services are conducted each Sunday by Dr. Cal Chambers, assisted on occasions by Mr. Jack Duckworth, a theology student at Regent College. The organists are Mrs. Eleanor Fenney and Mrs. Alice Chambers. Worship is conducted on Sundays at 10:30 AM.

WMS Fall Rally, 1953 (Kneeling, far right) Rev. Malcolm Blackburn, pastor

42. CALVIN PRESBYTERIAN CHURCH — ABBOTSFORD

The earliest record of a Presbyterian minister in this area dates back to 1878 when the Rev. Dr. Alexander Dunn visited Abbotsford–Matsqui on horseback. His ministry extended from Fort Langley to Hope and he often stayed with the Maclure family when in the Matsqui area.

By 1907 a student minister, Rev. John Alder, who had emigrated from England, took over the ministry, using a one-room schoolhouse on the corner of Laurel and Montvue.

The first Presbyterian church was built on Essendene shortly thereafter. In 1925, however, the Presbyterians joined the Methodist and Congregational churches to form the first Trinity Memorial United Church.

This left a void until 1941 when the Rev. H. Funston, minister of Cooke's Presbyterian Church in Chilliwack, (who was conducting the wedding of Julius Berki and Joan Egri) inquired into the matter. Although there were many Presbyterians among the Hungarian population, the area had no regular minister and no Presbyterian Church.

In 1945 a young Hungarian student minister, Kalman Doka, who spoke both Hungarian and English fluently, served briefly. The Rev. Funston continued to conduct English language services at the Orange Hall and occasionally a Hungarian minister from Calgary, the Rev. Dr. E. N. Molnar, conducted Hungarian language services.

In 1946 the members, largely Hungarians, elected a board of managers, and in conjunction with the Session of Cooke's Presbyterian Church in Chilliwack, recommended that a congregation be formed in Abbotsford and named "Calvin Presbyterian Church." On December 8 of that year the first Session was elected, the founding members being Julius Keis and Joseph Egri. Louis Szabo became a member of Session the following January. Julius Keis, a member of both the board of managers and Session, initiated the building of a Presbyterian Church in Abbotsford. A suitable site on Bourquin Crescent was purchased for $650, but unfortunately Julius died before the building was completed The Presbyterian Church, which had cost $4,222, was dedicated on July 10, 1949. The Rev. F.C. Funston officiated, assisted by Rev. Orth Gyozo.

Since there was no regular minister, visiting ministers and student ministers filled in between 1948 and 1950. In 1948 a Hungarian-speaking American student, Kalman Sulzok, served and taught seventeen young people who were confirmed at Cooke's Church later that year.

In 1950 the congregation called the Rev. Kalman (Kal) C. Doka as its first pastor. He arrived in Abbotsford on August 4 and two days later, preached his first sermon as minister to 65 people.

Initially, the Dokas lived on Elm Street. But when the family increased to seven, with the arrival of twin girls, they moved to a large house on the corner of Walnut Street. This house still stands and has a commanding view of Matsqui Prairie.

The Rev. Doka conducted the services in Hungarian, counselled his Hungarian-speaking members in the practices and traditions of an English-speaking Synod and Presbytery and worked toward the integration of both groups within the church family. His wife, Mary Ann, worked with the Hungarian ladies and with the English-speaking Women's Missionary Society, and also organized the Young Peoples' Society.

In 1952 the first English language service was conducted and the English part of the congregation grew. In 1956 Sam Norris was elected as the first English-speaking elder. That year the uprising in Hungary was followed by a massive immigration of refugees to Canada. Abbotsford received its share of refugees and the minister's house on Walnut Street became a temporary haven for the newcomers.

In 1958 a 16-foot by 20-foot extension was built on to the front of the church. Men and boys of the congregation provided much volunteer labour.

In March 1962 the Rev. Kal Doka accepted a call to Knox Church, Calgary. At his final service the hymns were sung in English and Hungarian simultaneously. The congregation hoped to replace the Rev. Doka with another bilingual minister and Dr. W. O. Nugent was appointed as interim moderator of Calvin Church Session until such a person could be found.

The Rev. Sandor Meszaros Jr. served for a short time before his appointment to Vancouver. In September 1963 the Rev. Robert M. Pollock, who did not speak Hungarian, was appointed, subject to finding a bilingual minister.

In 1966 the Rev. Sandor Meszaros Sr., who had recently retired from the Reformed Church of Hungary, was appointed as Pulpit Supply to serve the declining Hungarian-speaking membership.

In 1963 the board of managers replaced the manse on Walnut Street, with a new one on Plaxton Crescent. In September, the Rev. Pollock, together with his parents, moved in.

Calvin Church did not always have a regular organist or choir leader; Beverly Crocker served as church organist from 1952 to 1958. Mrs. Florence Garnet filled in until illness forced her to give up this post. In October 1963, Mrs. Belle Anderson, who had directed the United Church choir, was successfully recruited.

In 1958 Peter Crocker donated his old real estate office to the congregation and it served as a Sunday school building for many years. In 1970 the basement was refurbished, but since the work was still incomplete at the time of the 25th anniversary in 1971, the dinner was held at Trinity Memorial United Church.

The Rev. Robert Pollock left in April 1977, after 14 years of ministry here. The Rev. Harry Bailey served from April 16, 1978 until 1980.

Our present minister, the Rev. Donald Caron, commenced his ministry at Calvin in January 1981. As the area grew, so did our congregation. In 1983 two houses and our old Sunday school building were removed and a new sanctuary with nursery, lower hall, kitchen, and storage area was constructed. The new building was consecrated on September 29, 1985.

The Hungarian services continued from 1971 to 1984, led by the Hungarian-speaking minister, the Rev. S. Meszaros Jr. By that time, the Hungarian congregation had dwindled. The last Hungarian service was preached on January 6, 1985 and Calvin became an English-speaking congregation.

Our "Bells of Praise" handbell group, was formed in 1988 and is directed by our organist, Mrs. Lorraine Loewen. This dedicated, talented group provides excellent music whenever it participates in a service.

Calvin Presbyterian Church, 2597 E. Bourquin Crescent

A youth group, "Presbyteens" was formed in 1990. Mrs. Debbie L'Ecuyer leads this active and vibrant group in weekly study periods and social activities.

The programs in our friendly congregation also include the Prayer Chain group, Bible study groups, Ladies Guild, Small Wheels (a ladies group), choir and Sunday school.

Our services are held every Sunday morning at 10 AM. A very warm welcome is extended to all.

43. BETHEL REFORMED CHURCH

The Reformed Church originated at the time of the Reformation. Early settlers from Europe organized a Reformed Church in the New World as early as 1628. It is the oldest Protestant denomination with a continuous history in North America.

In the early 1950's, three families: the B. Schurers, the J. Van Tilborgs and the G. Waardenburgs, visited other Dutch families in the area, who might be interested in worshipping God according to the Reformed Church faith. Rev. Ten Zijthoff, the pastor of Hope Reformed Church in Vancouver, was asked to preach on Sunday evening December 11, 1954. They rented the Baptist Church in Matsqui Village and began worshipping there. The First Reformed Church of Lynden provided hymn books, church furniture and leadership in song service.

The first pastor, Rev. H. J. Boekhoven from Edmonton, preached his inaugural sermon January 20, 1957. Bethel purchased the old Abbotsford Pentecostal Church on Laurel and Montrose and began worshipping there,

Bethel Reformed Church met at Matsqui Baptist Church 1954-1957

with dedication of the building on August 11, 1957. A parsonage on Mayfair was purchased for $13,400.00.

In September, 1961, a farewell evening was held for Pastor and Mrs. Henry Boekhoven. Then Rev. and Mrs. Henry Franken accepted a call to this ministry and were received by Classis of Cascades on October 13, 1961. They left to become managers of Kirkside Inc. Rlbury, New York effective April 1, 1964. On August 14, 1964, Rev. Frank DeVries was installed as pastor and teacher. They left June 11, 1976 to pastor the Presbyterian Church in Wick, Ontario. Rev. and Mrs. LeRoy Sandee began their work at Bethel Nov. 19, 1976.

To initiate the construction of a new church, the parsonage was sold and the monies applied towards the property on Gladwin Road. Plans for our present building were approved on September 29, 1980. Hank Appeldoorn supervised the construction. The Laurel and Montrose church building was sold to Abbotsford Supply and Installation April 19, 1981. The Gladwin Church was dedicated on November 1, 1981.

Our church is known in the area by the stained glass window in the

front. The window entitled, "Job on the Dunghill" represents the trial of Job. God allowed Satan to take all the worldly goods from Job, and at the summit of this trial, he led the three friends to Job to tempt and console him. In Job 2:11 the friends come to Job

Bethel Reformed Church, Laurel & Montrose, 1957–1981

and in chapter 42 verse 9, they leave. Here God shows the victory of the one who holds on to Him, led by the Holy Ghost in the form of a dove. This window and the bell were donated by Mr. and Mrs. Karel Van Voorst Vader. Karel, an antique dealer died in the Lord December 16, 1986.

In October 1982, Pastor LeRoy and wife Elvira Sandee moved to Kings, Illinois, to serve the church there. A new shepherd for Bethel's flock, Pastor John Strik and wife Corrie arrived. He was installed September 22, 1983. We experienced growth and asked for help in our youth department. July 1, 1986, a student from Western Theological Seminary, William Wensink and wife Kathy arrived to serve for one year. During their stay, Bethel Church hired Bill become our youth pastor after his final year at seminary. He was installed on September 22, 1988.

For 23 years, Mrs. P. Madderom has served as church organist with unfailing and outstanding dedication.

The membership of Bethel Church and its outreach in the community is increasing steadily. During the past years the following groups have used our facilities: Bethesda for the Handicapped, A.A. group, Al Anon group, Kiwanis, Burden Bearers, Boy Scouts and Cubs. Many couples have been united in marriage in our beautiful sanctuary. Our pastors attend the MAMA and are interested in community affairs.

Arline Verdonk

Bethel Reformed Church, 3268 Gladwin Road

128

44. ABBOTSFORD CANADIAN REFORMED CHURCH

The members of the Abbotsford Canadian Reformed Church (at the corner of King and MacKenzie) understand better than their average neighbour what adjustment this modern world demands.

When the church was organized February 24, 1961, most of its members were new Canadians who had immigrated from the Netherlands after World War Two. They had experienced war and peace, rationing and plenty, learning to speak and think in a second language; religious persecution and freedom of worship.

But the history of their struggle with the modern world dates back to the confrontation between Holland and Spain in 1568. At that time a group of Dutch churches, under the influence of John Calvin's teachings, discussed matters of common concern. Due to cruel persecution in

Abbotsford Canadian Reformed Church, McKenzie & King Roads

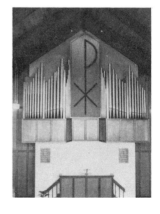

Holland, they met in Wessel, Germany and subsequently established the federation of Reformed Churches.

Dutch origins in North America can be traced back to the founding of New York (old New Amsterdam). The Reformed Church in America stems from the congregation established there in 1623.

After the Second World War many new arrivals from Holland worked on Canadian farms. Though new Canadians of Dutch origin had long been associated with the Christian Reformed Church and the Protestant Reformed Church, some of them felt a strong commitment to the liberation of the church in the Netherlands in 1944.

Children present retirement "gifts" to Rev. & Mrs. VanderWel

It was a return to a really reformed community, bound to the Scriptures and to the Three Forms of Unity and the accepted Church Order, bound to Christ Jesus. A group of Dutch immigrants in Lethbridge, Alberta, formed the Free Reformed Church on April 16, 1950.

On the advice of Rev. J. Hetinga from the Netherlands, who attended a meeting of the Lethbridge church on June 18, 1950, this group adopted the name Canadian Reformed Church. Within weeks, another church was instituted in Edmonton, and by mid-August others began at Georgetown, Ontario and Neerlandia, Alberta. The first Canadian Reformed Church in British Columbia was organized at New Westminster on December 17, 1950.

Former minister, Rev. M. Vanderwel, now retired, gives this interpretation of why the church chose the name it did: "Having immigrated to this country we should become Canadians and not stay by ourselves and retain only Dutch traditions. Furthermore, the nation benefits when the reformed faith is propagated."

Canadian Reformed Churches have never seen spectacular growth, either in Canada or British Columbia, but the increase has been steady.

Most Dutch settlements in B.C. are concentrated in the Fraser Valley where they have had a tremendous influence on agricultural development. Besides Surrey (formerly New Westminster) with 430 members, there are now Canadian and American Reformed Churches in Cloverdale, Langley, Chilliwack and Abbotsford. Together they support "The Voice of the Church" over radio station KARI (550 AM) every Sunday.

The Abbotsford congregation drew its membership not only from Canada but also from neighbouring communities in Everson, Lynden and Sumas, Washington. The U.S. members eventually formed the American Reformed Church of Lynden, Wa. Most of them are farmers and the well kept appearance of their land and buildings is silent testi-

Church Choir

mony to industry and prosperity. The present membership of the Abbotsford congregation stands at 545. The consistory is made up of ten elders and four deacons. Due to the retirement of Rev. M. VanderWel in December, 1991, we are in the process of calling a minister.

The weekly Sunday morning worship service begins at 10:00 AM and the afternoon service at 2:00 PM. The young people receive catechetical instruction on Tuesday and/or Wednesday nights. Members of the church are involved in activities such as Bible study groups, Men's and Women's Societies and choir.

The Canadian Reformed Churches of Abbotsford and Chilliwack, and the American Reformed Church at Lynden, WA. operate the John Calvin School in Yarrow, B.C. for grades 1–7, while students of high school age attend the Credo Christian High School in Langley.

Christmas program by students of John Calvin School

45. Abbotsford Seventh-Day Adventist Church

In 1928 Theodore and Dora Lapchevich and the Larsen family moved into the Aldergrove–Abbotsford area to work in the mill on Ross Road. Mr. Kanochky, another Seventh-day Adventist, soon joined the group and acted as their minister. They met in a large empty house at the corner of Ross and Maclure Roads. In 1932 the group organized as the Aldergrove Seventh-day Adventist Church.

In 1943 they bought some land on the corner of Mt. Lehman and Old Yale Roads, where they built a church. When cold weather set in, they installed a wood furnace under it.

In 1949, volunteers built a school room on the side of the church. Miss Dorothy Richardson (now Mrs. Mel Rowse) was the first teacher with ten students.

When the freeway came through, the government expropriated the church site. With the financial compensation from the government, the congregation built another church 200 yards to the south, on Mt. Lehman Road. Teacher Wally Serack acted as foreman while other members did the construction work.

Due to the influx of members into the Abbotsford–Clearbrook area, the church at Mt. Lehman became too small.

Former SDA Church, 2808 Mt. Lehman Road, dedicated Feb. 13, 1960 (now First Memorial Funeral Services)

Headquarters of the Seventh-day Adventist Churches of British Columbia and the Yukon

Abbotsford is home for the headquarters office of the Seventh-day Adventist Churches of British Columbia and the Yukon. The administrative complex is located at the corner of King and McCallum Roads.

On April 6, 1974 services began in the chapel of the B.C. Conference of Seventh-day Adventists on King and McCallum Roads. On September 7 of that year, the Abbotsford Seventh-day Adventist Church was formally organized with Matt Weststrate as pastor and 31 charter members. By December, four more members joined the church, making a total of 35. In December the church board voted to set up a new Church Building Fund.

In January 1975 the Abbotsford and Clearbrook congregations merged, bringing the combined membership to 81. The first meeting was held January 18.

Although the church board purchased the present site at 1921 Griffiths Road, it took several years before a building could be erected. In the meantime, the church met at the conference chapel until 1978 and then became tenants of St. Matthew's Anglican Church until December 1980.

The Abbotsford congregation conducted its first meeting in the new but unfinished building on February 14, 1981. When the building was completed and paid for, it was dedicated on January 26, 1985. On February 16, 1991, the church celebrated the tenth anniversary of worshipping at its present location.

Groundbreaking for the Abbotsford SDA Church, April 1979

Abbotsford SDA Church, 1921 Griffiths Road

46. GLADWIN HEIGHTS UNITED CHURCH

In April 1979, when a Fraser Presbytery Report indicated a possible need for a new church in the Abbotsford–Matsqui area, Trinity Memorial United Church established a Church Expansion Committee.

In November 1980 Trinity Memorial congregation approved a motion requesting B.C. Conference Development Committee to purchase property on Gladwin Road. The congregation pledged $20,000 per annum for five years to support the project.

A New Church Development Committee was formed to develop plans for a building site and establish a new congregation in the western part of Abbotsford–Matsqui. The first service of the new congregation was held September 13, 1981 at W. J. Mouat Senior Secondary School with approximately 30 people in attendance.

Original congregation of Gladwin Heights United, 1982

The Reverends Bob Gorrie and Bob Stobie of Trinity Memorial assisted Rev. Barry Moore and student interns Donna Jacques, Maureen Ashfield and Wendy Bily provided the ministry at this time.

Taking the name of Gladwin Heights, the congregation grew and flourished, with some 75 families attending Sunday services regularly. In 1983 the elected Steering Committee, chaired by Frank Bogle, adopted a Church Council Format with sub-committees for worship, Christian education, finance, building and maintenance, new church development, plus United

U.C.W. Ladies, March, 1983

Church Women and Presbytery reps. Dave McLaren was named chairperson.

On February 27, 1983, the building project began with the turning of the sod by Sarah Griffiths and Jim Degeer. The first service of worship in the new multi-purpose building was held September 12, 1983. The sanctuary was full. At this time the ministry was still provided by the team at Trinity Memorial. Others who assisted us during the formative years were: Barry Moore, Wes Bray, Jim Ford, Frank Golightly, George Fuller, Del Johnstone, Theo Roberts and Hartwell Illsey.

In the spring of 1985, Gladwin decided to ask Fraser Presbytery if we might become a separate congregation apart from Trinity Memorial. At the request of the congregation, Rev. Scott Agur was appointed interim minister. A year later, he was called to be our permanent minister. During the fall of 1986, Henri Locke was appointed part-time interim minister for a four-month period. Scott served us until June 1989, when he was called to a church in Sarnia, Ontario.

Turning of the Sod, February, 1983

Gladwin Heights United Church, 3474 Gladwin Road

In June 1989, the Pastoral Relations Committee recommended Rev. Art Lucy as our present minister, so he became part of the next chapter of Gladwin's history. While he was recovering from heart surgery, Sarah Wallace filled in as part-time interim minister from November 1990 to January 1991.

Rev. Lucy left Gladwin Heights April 30, 1992, and a new pastoral relationship began July 1, 1992.

Arlene Kropp

Rev. Art Lucy with the children

47. MOUNT LEHMAN UNITED CHURCH

On March 15, 1894, Mount Lehman Church was opened by the early pioneers who came from Prince Edward Island, Nova Scotia, Quebec and Ontario in the 1800's. Soon afterward, a large tree fell on the church and it had to be rebuilt. The church was constructed of hand-hewn timbers that still provide a solid base for the original structure.

The pioneers included Methodists, Presbyterians, Baptists and Anglicans, who formed a Union Church. Ministers of different denominations conducted Sunday services on an alternating basis. In 1904 the church was taken over by the Presbyterians. By a majority vote of members in 1925, the congregation joined the newly formed United Church of Canada, thus fulfilling the wish of the original founders to include everyone in their service.

Following the vote of Union, Mount Lehman Church became part of a four point pastoral charge. Since Mount Lehman had a manse, it was the main part of this pastoral charge. The other small churches were Clayburn, Poplar and Pine Grove. The minister had no transportation.

Mt. Lehman United Church, 6256 Mt. Lehman Road

After two or three years of accepting horse and buggy rides from church members, he purchased a car, which he parked in the horse barn at the church.

As time went on, Clayburn Church left the pastoral charge to join St. Andrew's United Church in Mission, and Poplar Church joined Trinity United Church in Abbotsford. Mount Lehman Church and Pine Grove Church remained a two point pastoral charge until the latter was closed, approximately 1960. This left Mount Lehman alone, which was an impossible position financially. After approaching Abbotsford, Langley and Fort Langley to no avail, Aldergrove United Church came forward and accepted Mount Lehman Church as its "little sister."

Mount Lehman is forever thankful to Aldergrove for keeping them from becoming a "has been" church! After 28 years of support and friendship, Aldergrove and Mount Lehman United churches are moving apart and becoming independent pastoral charges on July 1, 1992.

Each congregation wishes the other spiritual growth and blessings as we each accept God's challenge to provide worship and fellowship for our individual communities.

48. Trinity Memorial United Church

In 1874, as one of the two ministers of the Presbyterian Church in the whole of British Columbia, Robert Jamieson went to Scotland and arranged that four ministers be sent out from the "Old Kirk" to begin their ministry in the newest province. Alex Dunn was sent out in 1875 to the part of Jamieson parish that extended from the village of Yale to the mouth of the Fraser River. He ministered to the congregations in the Fraser Valley until he retired in 1905.

Rev. John Charles Alder from England was appointed to Abbotsford in April, 1907. Since there was no Presbyterian Church building in Abbotsford, Rev. Alder began the ambitious project of raising funds and enthusiasm to build their first church on Essendene. By February 1908 it as opened debt-free!

Rev. J. L. Campbell and his wife came to Abbotsford in April 1910, and oversaw the building of the manse, completed in 1911. Within eight months, he and his wife made 300 calls on local people. Besides the services in Abbotsford, he conducted meetings in Huntingdon or Musselwhite on alternate Sundays. Before Sumas Lake was drained, the ideal place for the church picnic was at Belrose, a train stop on the south side of the big lake. After the lake was drained, picnics were arranged at places like White Rock, Birch Bay, and Lynden, Washington.

Presbyterian Church on Essendene, 1908

Soon the little church was too small for the congregation, and in 1913 an addition was planned. A few years after that, the church basement was sunk under the existing main building. In 1946, during the strongest earthquake this region has yet felt, the Sunday School children walked, singing, from this basement to see the telephone and light wires sway like skipping ropes outside the church! As long as the old church stood, the gold letters of the words: "God is Love," shone down on the congregation from the wall behind the pulpit.

In 1917, Rev. Campbell resigned to make room for someone with greater physical energies. By January 1918, Rev. W. Robertson was the new minister for Abbotsford. Scourges of mosquitoes plagued the area in 1921 causing illnesses that affected church and Sunday School attendance. In 1922 Sumas Lake was drained and reclaimed, eliminating part of the enormous breeding ground for the pests.

Rev. G. S. Paton served our church from 1925 through 1932. In the year of his arrival, discussions of Church Union with the Methodist and Congregational Churches were under way, to form the United Church of Canada! Votes were taken in every congregation throughout the nation. In Abbotsford, 35 favoured Church Union and 5 decided they would rather not take that step. When the union was about to be consummated later that year, Elder Alex MacCallum (after whom McCallum Road is named), proposed that since three churches (Abbotsford, Huntingdon and Poplar) were to be united, the name "Trinity" would be appropriate.

From 1932 through 1937 the much loved and admired Rev. Moses served the Abbotsford congregation. He was followed by Rev. Cameron in 1938, the year that the Huntingdon church was closed. Trinity Church was newly painted and in 1942, upon Rev. Cameron's retirement, Rev. Tench and his family took charge.

In 1944, when a census regarding church affiliation was taken in the M.S.A. area, 288 families expressed their preference for the United Church. Talk turned to building a new church and rough sketches were drawn. After the war, actualization of these plans was approached with new vigour. On June 18, 1947, the cornerstone of the new Trinity Memorial Church was laid. The following summer, with the shell of the superstructure complete, the new minister, Rev. A. L. Elliott dedicated the building. Services were conducted in the basement for two years, until the interior was finished.

When the old church was no longer needed, the building was sold to the Roman Catholic Church, who moved it to the corner of Hazel and Gladys to serve as an addition to their sanctuary. The old property, the present site of the Saan store, was sold.

In 1950 Trinity United celebrated the 25th anniversary of Church Union. On the last Sunday in September, 1951, the new church was dedicated. Rev. Elliott resigned in 1954 and Rev. H. P. Collins accepted the ministerial calling of Trinity. By 1956, church membership had doubled from 1946, and Sunday School attendance had tripled!

In 1955 Mrs. Margaret Weir, who had come to the church in 1912, was appointed dean of women at the Naramata Winter Session. Her appointment exemplified the increasing responsibilities being given to women in the church organization. A student who attended at that session, Bob Stobie, became a minister of Trinity in 1979.

On May 12, 1957, at sod-turning for the new Youth Centre, the youngest and oldest members of the congregation jointly held the spade.

New church under construction at Hazel & Montrose, 1947

In January, 1960, Rev. Collins resigned and in July, Rev. W. R. B. Nixon and his wife came to serve at Trinity. Led by Mrs. Nixon and her daughter, the Explorers and the CGIT (Canadian Girls in Training) provided many community services. The 1960's proved to be growing years for the church.

In 1962 the UCW, a union of the former Women's Auxiliary and Women's Missionary Society, was inaugurated. In 1966 Rev. Nixon moved to Sardis United Church and Rev. Hadden Gregory occupied the manse on Clark Drive. Under his leadership the Session met more often and plans were drawn up for "Every Family Visitation" in 1968. A church newsletter was published for the first time and a church secretary manned the office Tuesdays through Fridays. Prior to 1970, people voiced the need for an assistant minister.

Rev. Gregory pioneered the introduction of Special Education programs in local schools. From September 1970 until June 1972, congregational life was enriched by the presence of Deaconess Edythe Stocton. With a large influx of young married couples from Vancouver in the early 1970's, the nursery and three-year-old activity areas had to be expanded!

In June 1973, Rev. Gregory resigned and was replaced by Rev. Ben Taylor who thought he was coming to a small, quiet country church! Instead, he found a church in the middle of a population explosion.

During the renovation that removed the balcony and remodelled the sanctuary in 1974, services were conducted at the Old Age Pensioners' Hall. Since Trinity had provided facilities for the pensioners during the construction of their hall, the latter happily reciprocated, at no charge. The Clarke Drive manse was sold to help raise funds for the renovation.

Trinity Memorial United Church, 33737 Hazel 1975

When the work was completed the following spring, dedication services were held April 27, 1975.

After Rev. Taylor underwent major heart surgery in 1976, a team ministry involving Rev. Bob Stobie was instituted in 1979. Although he retired from full-time ministry in 1980, Rev. Taylor continues to use his talents at Trinity. That year the daughter congregation, Gladwin Heights United Church opened its doors. Rev. Bob Gorrie and Rev. Stobie served both churches until 1984, when Stobie resigned. In 1985 Rev. Douglas Ireland arrived at Trinity and Rev. Scott Agur at Gladwin Heights. Rev. Hartwell Illsey assisted part-time in 1985, while lay minister Doug Astle served in 1986–87. Rev. Clayton Arkesteyn-Vogler served in a team ministry 1987–88, before going to Hope United Church. Rev. Stuart Lyster ministered in that capacity for the next two years, until he went to White Rock United Church.

Mrs. Diane Cardin came as lay minister in summer 1990, was ordained in May 1991 and called to Oak Street United Church in Vancouver. In July 1991, Rev. Clayton Arkesteyn-Vogler returned to Trinity's team ministry with Rev. Ireland.

Today, Abbotsford finds itself in a situation similar to the 1970's, with a growing number of families moving in from Vancouver. Many groups meet in the halls of Trinity Memorial United Church. The CGIT group is beginning again, and the youth group is very active. Two choirs, a highly involved UCW membership, a committed men's group and countless other activities appear on the schedule as Trinity faithfully participates in spiritual growth in Abbotsford.

49. Abbotsford Christian Assembly

Abbotsford Christian Assembly, on Gladwin at Downes, was founded in the spring and summer of 1956 by two young women from Glad Tidings in Vancouver.

Congregation of Glad Tidings Tabernacle, 1957 (later Abbotsford Christian Assembly)

Meetings were held in the Odd Fellows Hall in Abbotsford. Their theme was, "There's Revival in the Air Today." They started with services on Tuesday evenings and Sunday mornings. Pastor R. Layzell, of Vancouver Glad Tidings, held special meetings bringing the message of praise and worship.

After one year the small fellowship, known at that-time as Glad Tidings Tabernacle, moved into a storefront on South Fraser Way. It was known as a warm, friendly church right from the start. Many changes occurred as various pastors came and went. The church grew slowly but steadily those first few years.

In August of 1960, construction began on a permanent facility on Gladwin Road about two miles south of our present building. Everyone, including many from Vancouver, became involved in building our own place of worship. A great celebration was held in January 1961 to dedicate our new facility. A steeple was added to the building in 1969 which greatly enhanced the appearance of the structure.

By the spring of 1971 the fellowship had grown to approximately 60. At this time our present pastor, David McElhoes, his wife Vi, and their four children arrived to pastor our growing church.

The fellowship continued to grow under the ministry of Pastor McElhoes. Roy Rubuliak, currently an associate pastor, and his wife, Betty, joined us in 1975.

In February 1978, Logos Fellowship, pastored by Dr. Henry Lindberg, joined our congregation. That year we also started our Christian School. We began with 45 students and Dr. Lindberg as our first principal.

In 1979 we felt it was important to relate more to the community in which we lived. The congregation decided to change the name of the fellowship to Abbotsford Christian Assembly.

An annex was added to our existing building but it soon became necessary to look for a larger piece of property. In 1980, 9.7 acres of land were purchased on the corner of Gladwin and Downes. Work on the new building commenced in September 1980. The new building was completed in March 1981. Our school, Abbotsford Christian Academy, moved to the upstairs rooms.

The little house that was on the property has been moved to the back corner. It currently serves as the residence of our full-time custodian.

In April 1984 another fellowship, All Nations Christian Fellowship, pastored by Tom Tutyko, and his wife, Irene, joined us. Tom is now our full-time missionary evangelist.

The church continued to grow under the leadership of Pastor McElhoes. In June 1990 we broke ground for our new multipurpose building. This unique new building connected to our original structure serves not only as a complete gymnasium with a full-sized basketball court but also as an attractive auditorium that seats 1,000.

Our new "gymnatorium" has a high tech rubber floor and a sound sys-

Inside Gymnatorium

Abbotsford Christian Assembly with Church Offices and Christian Academy Complex

tem able to handle almost any type of concert or performances. It also has a large stage with motorized curtain for drama presentations. It is a completely practical and yet beautiful building that is in constant use. Our Academy makes good use of the gym as do many other groups within the church.

Our church presently has a congregation of 650 and is steadily growing. We offer many varied programs including: nursery, Sunday School, Kidz Club, boys and girls clubs, Junior Young People's, Teens Alive, College and Careers, Young Marrieds, Home Bible Study Groups, Bible College, Seniors Fellowship, Prayer Services, Care Groups, Widows Fellowship and Christian School.

The church has a staff of three full-time pastors, one full-time missionary evangelist, one full-time administrator, one full-time secretary, one part-time special projects person, one part-time bookkeeper, one full-time custodian and one part-time custodian.

Our school has 152 students and a staff of 29. Our school principal is Blair McHenry.

Abbotsford Christian Assembly operates under Christian Outreach of Canada, a registered society. Our vision is to provide a warm, friendly church that encourages and equips its members for Christian ministry and as ambassadors for Christ.

Our outreach vision is first to our own area and ultimately to our whole country. Spirit West in Vancouver is the first outreach church originating from Christian Assembly. Pastor Tim Klassen and his wife, Virginia, were sent out by Christian Assembly along with another couple, Bill and Vivienne Conway, to reach out to the people of Vancouver.

Foreign missions work includes the Philippines, Mexico, Poland, the Ukraine and Taiwan. The primary purpose is to hold crusades in conjunction with national churches as well as seminars for national pastors and church leaders.

50. Covenant Fellowship

Covenant Fellowship has been a part of the Clearbrook community for eight years, though a large portion of this group of people have been fellowshipping together for some twenty years.

ORIGINS

During the "Jesus Movement" and the "Charismatic Movement" of the late 1960's and early 1970's, the movement of the Holy Spirit brought people from all different denominations together to praise and worship God. They formed the beginning of the body of people at Surrey Christian Centre, under the leadership of Rev. Ern Baxter, a familiar figure in the Vancouver area. He was the former pastor of the Evangelistic Tabernacle, Vancouver, later becoming a much sought-after conference speaker. As Rev. Baxter's ministry grew and his travelling time increased, the leadership of Christian Centre was passed on to elders of the church.

When the Surrey Christian Centre ended at the beginning of the 1980's, a new, smaller church called Covenant Fellowship was formed under the leadership of Rev. Howard Carter. He also pastored churches in Australia and has since gone home to be with the Lord. During that time Covenant Fellowship maintained indirect leadership from Rev. Baxter. Under God's leading, the church moved to the Abbotsford area in 1984 and purchased the Country Inn Motel in Clearbrook. That served as a Bible college for a few years, attended by students from B.C. and Australia.

As more of the families in the church moved to the Clearbrook–Abbotsford area, the Sunday services were moved to rented facilities in Clearbrook. For the past four years, Covenant Fellowship's meetings have been held in the Clearbrook Community Centre on Clearbrook Road, to whom we are indeed grateful.

UP TO THE PRESENT

The pastor of Covenant Fellowship in Henry Desjarlais, who with his family has been a member of the church for over 20 years. The church has no ties with the Discipleship Movement or any other denomination. We are an independent local church of about 160 people, seeking closer fellowship with other local churches. Pastor Henry is a member of the local MAMA (Matsqui–Abbotsford Ministerial Association), as well as the CMA (Christian Ministers Association) which includes pastors from the lower mainland and other parts of western Canada.

OUTREACH

We support the Youth for Christ's ministry in this area, as well as other needs. In spring 1992 the pastor and a group of men will travel to Romania as part of an outreach team to preach the Gospel there and to work with and support an orphanage. We also support the church in the Philippines through the work of Rev. Colin Shaw, a missionary to that country.

Rev. Henry & Mrs. Desjarlais

Through God's grace and the Lord's dealings over these 20 years, this fellowship of committed families is becoming a stronger local church within a community, with a heart for outreach and sharing the Gospel of Jesus Christ to the lost.

Covenant Fellowship meets for worship Sunday mornings at 10:30 and provides Sunday school for children ages 2 through 8, as well as a nursery. We are looking for a piece of property or a building that will suit our needs in the future. Clearbrook is our home. The Lord planted us here and we want to be a blessing to the Body of Christ here, as well as to the community at large.

As a part of the larger Body of Christ we consider the single most important underlying factor of our being to be the promise we have of: Immanuel, God is with us, and He has never failed us yet. In Him we rejoice!

51. FAMILY WORSHIP CENTRE

On March 4, 1979, at the home of Don & Alma Harter, 1881 Dahl Crescent, Ron & Bernice Nelson shared their vision for starting a local church and Bible training centre in the community of Abbotsford–Matsqui.

Ron & Bernice Nelson

More than a dozen enthusiastic adults attended that meeting, thus beginning a new fellowship in the community. Before long, God gave favour and increase to this humble beginning and a new facility had to be found to accommodate all the people who were being committed to this fellowship. The first temporary location for meeting was the Key Hotel banquet room (now Park Hotel), then the McCallum Activity Centre for a short season, followed by the Memorial Funeral Home on Mt. Lehman Road. It became obvious that a more per-

Family Worship Centre, 2413 McCallum Road

manent place was needed, and on August 24, 1980, Family Worship Centre Society purchased a property and church building at 2413 McCallum Road (formerly the Nazarene Church), our present location.

The vision has always been to have a family oriented

Frank & Faith Wall

church reaching out to the community in various capacities. Family Worship Centre is committed to preaching the Good News of the Gospel to a lost and dying world and strives to work with other churches in this locale, knowing that we are only a part of the larger Body of Christ.

Our people have a strong desire to send missionaries to the uttermost parts of the earth. The Bible Training Centre which we incorporated as part of the church on September 8, 1980, trains men and women for short and long term missions. At present, graduates from the Bible Training Centre serve in countries like Guatemala, Hong Kong, Africa, Philippines, Ecuador, Malaysia, England and Switzerland.

Frank & Faith Wall, founding members and Dean of the Bible Training Centre, yearned to see small communities in British Columbia being affected by the Gospel of Jesus Christ. Subsequently, in 1986 they began a new work in the mixed ethnic community of Deroche, approximately 45 minutes northeast of Abbotsford, on the north side of the Fraser River. Therefore the Bible Training Centre has been temporarily put on hold. God willing, the work of training more students for the work of the Lord will be resumed in the near future.

One of the strong features for which the Family Worship Centre is known in this community is the

Don Harter

Ken & Sharlene Greter

praise and worship service held at the church every Sunday. Don Harter, one of the founding members has been one of the main contributors to the success of the worship services by leading the worship team for almost a decade.

The children's church of Family Worship Centre ministers on a regular basis to the elderly in the community. Various adult groups also serve senior citizens in their places of residence, encouraging them to remain strong in the Lord.

After six and a half years of pastoring, Ron & Bernice Nelson went into full-time ministry in the mission field, and pastoral duties were taken over by Ken & Sharlene Greter, the former youth pastor of the church.

Pastor Greter has a strong desire to see the children and the youth of our community strongly committed and zealous for the Lord, instead of entertaining the worldly philosophies and lurings that tempt so many of our younger generation today. To help strengthen the families in the local community, home fellowship meetings take place throughout the city during the course of each week, as an extension of the church.

Sunday services at Family Worship Centre are held at 10:00 AM and 6:30 PM, with mid-week services and youth meetings on Tuesday and Wednesday evenings. The heartbeat of Family Worship Centre is summarized by its logo which says, "As for me and my house, we will serve the Lord."

52. Prairie Chapel

In 1951, the late Albert Nickel and his wife Mary, from the West Abbotsford Mennonite Church, pioneered a Sunday school on Sumas Prairie to meet the spiritual needs of children living on the farms there. The work began in a private house, then moved to an abandoned, flood-damaged hut donated by Buckerfield's. After volunteers cleaned up the place, the facility was used until 1954. That fall, building was started on the present site and completed in March 1955. During these early years the teachers and other helpers drove around the Prairie picking up children for Sunday school.

Sumas Sunday School Mission, established by West Abbotsford Teachers (l.to r.): Susan Bartsch, Helen Sawatzky, Henry Wiebe, Jake Schellenberg, Lena Funk, Frank Sawatzky, Bert Nickel, Frieda Wiebe, Henry Krause, Mary Nickel, Jack Nickel

The work grew and by 1958 Dave and Phyllis Wiebe were called to pastor the work and evening services were begun. Children from local farms and different church backgrounds attended the clubs program each Friday night. Daily Vacation Bible schools were conducted during spring break and summer holidays. An annual highlight has always been the old fashioned Sunday school picnic.

In July 1960 Les and Lydia Friesen assumed the pastoral duties. Beginning in 1961 a school bus purchased from the Chilliwack School District was used transport young people and children. By this time a group of adults were attending regularly.

Prairie Chapel, 1969

In 1969 the mission work was officially organized as an independent church and changed its name from Sumas Sunday School Mission to Prairie Chapel. In 1970 a sanctuary was added, built mostly by volunteer labour and progressing as the money came in. Praise God, there was no interruption from April 1970 when the footings were poured, until October 18 when the Thanksgiving service was held in the new building.

In 1967 Bert Nickel took over as pastor and continued until 1972. For several years the work went on without a full-time pastor, but the congregation was assisted by Rev. H. P. Fast and Ken Thiessen, a student pastor. In the summer of 1973 a visitor from England, Martin Gouldthorpe, preached at one of the services. The congregation decided to ask this visitor and his wife Grace to become the pastor. The Gouldthorpes accepted the call and arrived on January 1, 1975.

During these years summer baptisms were held in the Sumas River at Hougan Park. With the growing congregation, weddings became a frequent occurrence and these were followed a while later by child dedications and a thriving children's church program.

By the early 1980's the congregation of Prairie Chapel felt the need either to expand the facilities or to relocate. After much prayer and consideration it was agreed to expand on the present site. To alleviate an immediate space problem in the Sunday school, a mobile unit was purchased and installed.

After 14 years of faithful service Martin Gouldthorpe resigned, having brought the church to the point where expansion was needed. Again it was agreed that the building would only proceed as the funds allowed.

In summer 1989 the old wing was pulled down and a new two-storey education wing was erected in its place. Many members of the congregation worked hard on the construction, along with the new pastor, Fred Tomlinson. Gordon and Betty Honen from Chilliwack lived in a trailer on the site and voluntarily supervised the construction for approximately six months. By the end of 1990 the new wing was completed and the renovations of the sanctuary began. The whole building project was completed without having to miss a Sunday service on this site and without borrowing any money. The present pastor, Rev. Bill Fullerton and his wife Barbara joined the work in September 1990.

Prairie Chapel may not be one of the largest churches in the area but this small and friendly congregation seeks to meet the needs of the outlying area of Sumas Prairie. Many of its congregation however, come from Abbotsford, Clearbrook and Yarrow. The church's ministry reaches out to many different areas of the world by supporting overseas missions and local missions. The areas are as diverse as Japan, Jordan, Papua New Guinea and closer to home Kilgard, Straiton and refugee work in Clearbrook.

At the recent dedication of the new facility the theme was, "To God be the glory, great things He has done." From the small beginnings in 1951 until the present, events at Prairie Chapel testify of the great things God has done.

Prairie Chapel, 1990

Church-Related Institutions

53. Abbotsford Christian School

Closely connected to the growth of the Christian Reformed Churches in the area was the development of the Abbotsford Christian School system.

For people of the Reformed persuasion, Christian education of their young is a must, not only in the home and church, but also in the day school. Consequently, only one month after the organization of the First CR Church on November 9, 1950, Mr. D. DeVries called to order a meeting to form the Abbotsford Christian School Society. Nineteen members signed up, a board was elected, and the society incorporated.

The school doors opened for the first year of operation on September 8, 1953 with approximately 75 pupils and a staff of 3 teachers in the basement of the church.

The following year, when the church began building the present First CR Church at the corner of McCallum and Holland Roads, the school took over the building and 13-acre property on Mission Highway.

First Building of Abbotsford Christian School

The Lord blessed the efforts and in spite of many difficulties and early make-shift facilities, the school grew. During the summer of 1960 a new four room school was built on the site of the present Heritage Campus. These four rooms survived the fire of 1985 and form part of the present school.

The school continued to grow rapidly through the 1960's and 1970's. Four more classrooms were built in 1966 and another three in 1967. During the early 1970's, the School Board began planning a high school to round out their Christian educational system. The property on Old Clayburn Road was bought and the Junior Secondary grades 8, 9, 10 were

Abbotsford Christian School, Heritage Campus

moved to this new location in 1976. In 1979 the Senior Secondary grades were started and the first students graduated from Grade 12 in June 1981.

The addition of kindergarten in September 1985 provided the final touch. The Society's goal of providing Christian education from kindergarten through grade 12 was now realized.

A major tragedy struck when almost the entire elementary school (with the exception of the four rooms mentioned earlier) was destroyed by fire on May 1, 1985. Rebuilding started immediately and on April 19, 1986 the new and improved Heritage Campus Elementary School was officially opened.

From 1986 to the present, the growth of the school has been phenomenal, mainly because many evangelical Christian parents have joined the Christian School Society and are sending their children to the school. The Society, from very humble beginnings, has become inter-denominational in scope and over 1000 children now receive their education in this God-centered school system.

The following are some recent developments.

1988: The first portables were added to the elementary school signalling that it had outgrown its newly expanded facilities. A band room/music complex was added to our high school, creating a facility to match the developments of the band program.

1990: The Abbotsford Christian School Society anxiously awaited permission to construct a second elementary campus (K–7) school campus on ten acres of land purchased in May 1989 behind Fraser Valley College.

1991: Unable to obtain re-zoning on its newly acquired McConnel Road property and faced with ever increasing enrolment pressures, the

New Clayburn Hills Campus

Abbotsford Christian School Society voted to purchase a different 10-acre site at 3939 Old Clayburn Road. Plans for the construction of a second elementary campus began immediately.

1991: Abbotsford Christian Elementary officially divided into two elementary campuses. The facility on the Mission Highway was renamed Abbotsford Christian School — Heritage Campus reflecting that this was the original site of the school, as well as the rich heritage of Christian principles upon which the school was established. The new elementary campus was named Abbotsford Christian School — Clayburn Hills Campus, reflecting its geographic location.

1992: In September 1992, the Abbotsford Christian School will enter its 40th year of operation as a Christian School in the Abbotsford–Matsqui community. Its three campus sites are home to over 1,000 students, making it one of the largest independent school systems in the province.

Abbotsford Christian Secondary School

54. Columbia Bible College

Bible schools in Canada began at the turn of the century. They developed out of a desire to have biblically literate laity in the church. They trained men and women to be missionaries and pastors who spread the Word of God in North America and other parts of the world.

Contemporary Canadian Bible colleges have retained the basic thrust of the early schools but have broadened the curriculum to include courses in English, History, Psychology, Philosophy, and Anthropology. The purpose of adding these subjects to the core curriculum of Bible and theology, is to provide a well rounded education. The effective Bible college helps the student develop thoughts and actions that are scripturally relevant to the mainstream of the world in which he or she lives and witnesses.

Original building of MB Bible School c. 1950

PREPARING PEOPLE FOR LIFE AND MINISTRY

Columbia Bible College in Clearbrook is a cooperative effort of the Mennonite Brethren and Conference of Mennonites in B.C. Each denomination had its own schools dating back to the 1930's. However, in 1970 they agreed to form one school — Columbia, at 2940 North Clearbrook Road.

Besides offering courses to

Bethel Bible Institute (CMinBC) c. 1960

almost 300 students each year, the college has a growing Continuing Education Department which offers seminars, workshops and evening classes to the community at large.

Under the motto "Preparing People for Life and Ministry," the on-campus programs include: a one year Certificate and two year Diploma program, as well as a four year Bachelor of Religious Education degree. Students may major in Biblical Studies, Church Ministries, or Mission. A new government approved program in Early Childhood

Students in front of administration building, 2940 Clearbrook Road

Education for preparing licensed Day Care workers was begun in 1991 and is drawing a growing number of students.

The program of Columbia seeks to fulfil at least four objectives: 1) to develop Christian character in the lives of students by means of prayer,

Men's Residence

classroom instruction, service, and community life; 2) to develop in students a Biblical worldview, applying Biblical principles to all areas of life; 3) to lay a foundation for lifelong learning, particularly in understanding and obeying Scripture; 4) to equip students for practical ministry in the church and in the world.

College age youth are a priceless resource for the church. People who are biblically literate and keen in life skills are a tremendous asset to our society. Columbia Bible College seeks to help prepare such people to fulfil their calling in the world.

Walter Unger, President

Music Ministry

New CBC Learning Resource Centre

55. Mennonite Educational Institute

The Mennonite Educational Institute (MEI) wants to be known as a school whose people are "on the move!" The school began in 1944 when the South Abbotsford Mennonite Brethren Church offered part of its Bible School facilities for use as a high school. Forty-three students in grades 9 to 11 formed the first MEI student body.

MEI 1946

MEI 1975

Provincial Basketball Championship, 1963

The MEI was a response of the Mennonite people in the Matsqui–Abbotsford area to the question, "How much are our youth worth to us?" The provincial government approved its establishment on the conditions that qualified teachers be employed, students write the same exams as public school students, and government funding not be expected. The founders of the school expanded these conditions to include teaching faith, ethics, heritage language, occupation, and citizenship.

MEI moved into its own new six-room school on the corner of Old Yale and Clearbrook Roads in 1946. In 1947 an auditorium-gymnasium and in 1954 a four-room junior high school were added. In 1970 a modern, large gymnasium was constructed, which is part of the Clearbrook Community Centre today. In 1980, the MEI, bearing the slogan, "MEI on the Move", built a modern, spacious campus on eighteen acres at the corner of the Clearbrook and Downes Roads. These premises have already undergone two expansions: six classrooms to the east-end (1988) and a new library, art laboratory, and two classrooms on the west-end (1992).

Since 1944 enrolment has increased to 690 (grades 8 to 12) today. During its forty-six years of operation, only eight principals have given administrative leadership: Franz Thiessen (1944–45), Isaac J. Dyck (1945–57), William A. Wiebe (1957–62), David H. Neumann (1962–69), Hugo Friesen (1969–79), Wally Sawatzky (1979–90), and Leo Regehr (1990–). These principals, together with many qualified and committed teachers, have kept the school in the forefront of educational developments. Today MEI is a group 1, government-funded school whose

MEI today

graduates are qualified for admission into universities, colleges, technical or vocational schools, and Bible Schools and Colleges.

Part of MEI's strength stems from its strong parental and church support. At the time of writing, MEI is sponsored by twelve Mennonite Churches: Arnold Community, Bakerview Mennonite Brethren, Cedar Valley Mennonite, Clearbrook MB, East Aldergrove MB, Eben-Ezer Mennonite, Emmanuel Mennonite, King Road MB, Mission Christian Fellowship, Northview Community, South Abbotsford MB and West Abbotsford Mennonite Church.

Another reason for the school's strength lies in variety of students who select MEI as their school. About one-third of the students are affiliated with sponsoring churches; one-third are affiliated with churches that do not sponsor the MEI; and one-third are from non-Mennonite churches or are not affiliated with any church at all. This creates a good atmosphere at the school and promotes cultural enrichment.

The MEI Board, its administration, and staff are still deeply committed to responding to the question, "How much are our youth worth to us?" The high value placed on youth is reflected in curricular offerings which are constantly expanded to keep pace with the expanding needs of young people. Accepting the guidelines of provincial curricula, MEI offers a wide range of courses in each of the curricular strands: Bible, the Humanities, the Sciences, Practical Arts, and the Fine Arts. The overriding objective is to develop young people physically, mentally, socially, and spiritually within the dimensions of a personal relationship with Jesus Christ, and thereby prepare students for a wholesome and purposeful life.

Wally Sawatzky

56. VALLEY CHRISTIAN SCHOOL
"…more than just a school"

Valley Christian School is an independent, co-educational, non-profit school that was given recognition by the Evaluation Team from the Ministry of Education in the spring of 1986. It recognized our distinctive philosophy and established that our educational standards met those of the ministry. This status qualified the school for the educational funding available from the B.C. government. The certificate of group classification was updated in 1990 to Group 1 (Primary through Grade 7).

VCS is a member of the Association of Christian Schools International (ACSI). This association gives professional assistance in developing the distinctively Christian dimensions of school operation and curriculum. (The ACSI has over 2,500 member schools in Canada, U.S. and forty nations overseas.)

One of the most important reasons for the effectiveness of Valley Christian School is the cooperation between home, church and school.

Christian families in this area felt the need for a school that supported the values of the Christian home. They had chosen churches that reinforced their family values, but the only way to have a school do this, was to establish one that was independent and committed to their Christian values.

Today Valley Christian School

includes families from over a dozen denominations. They are united in their commitment to fundamental matters of faith and practice, on which the Bible instruction and standards of the school are based. The home and church assume responsibility for giving instruction in denominational distinctives.

Consistent with this view of the home as the first and most important force in the education of children is the realization that there must be a partnership in instruction. Parents must be informed regarding the work of the school and stand ready to supplement it in various ways.

Valley Christian School opened its doors to 35 students in the fall of 1983. It provides education consistent with the Christian world-and-life view of the parents who brought it into being. As its program became known, enrollment grew to over 200. Additional campuses are operating in Mission and Chilliwack.

Families desiring to enroll their children must qualify and apply for admission to the school society. At least one parent must profess saving faith in Jesus Christ as Saviour and Lord, and both parents must support the spiritual, educational and behaviour standards of the school.

The policies and procedures under which the school operates are determined by the school board, whose members are elected annually by the school society. Each campus is directed by a principal, guided by policies the board establishes.

The staff members are chosen for their Christian testimony, professional preparation and commitment to support the standards of the school in their lives and families. VCS employs teachers who are certified by the Ministry of Education. All staff attend the annual Fall ACSI Northwest Teacher Convention in Portland, Oregon.

57. Western Pentecostal Bible College

The residential campus of Western Pentecostal Bible College is located at 35235 Straiton Road, on 101 acres of the sunset slopes of Sumas Mountain just above the historic village of Clayburn. The mountainside location, about halfway between Abbotsford and Mission, provides spectacular views from each of the campus buildings.

The founding and formative years of WPBC (originally called British Columbia Bible Institute) were spent in Victoria, where the fledgling college shared the facilities of the Glad Tidings Church (1941–1951).

Growth in enrollment forced the college to relocate to new facilities on St. Mary's Avenue in North Vancouver. With this move, it became a residential college, and in 1962 acquired its present name.

Administration Building

When the leadership realized that future development would require accommodations that might be restricted by urban by-laws, the present site was acquired in 1971.

New campus construction began in 1973, and the college took occupancy in the fall of 1974. The three original buildings were augmented by the Vernon Morrison Residence in 1977, and the P.S. Jones Memorial Auditorium in 1979. The Mary Ellen Anderson Memorial Chapel was built in 1986, and the Lorne Philip Hudson Memorial Library in 1988.

Although it accepts students from many denominations, Western Pentecostal Bible College is the theological college of the B.C. and

Yukon District of the Pentecostal Assemblies of Canada. There are over 150 affiliated churches in the district.

After the Annual District Conference of 1966 gave full endorsement for an expansion of the academic curriculum, the first stages of the additions were implemented. In March, 1967, the British Columbia provincial legislature granted the college a charter officially recognizing it as "a Theological College" and conferring upon it "the power to provide instruction in Theology, Religious Education and Sacred Music only." The Lieutenant Governor's proclamation to grant degrees, however, did not occur until June 1981.

The college curriculum was developed and refined, and the academic preparation of its faculty systematically advanced. The library was upgraded and the college board and academic senate were reorganized to conform to American Association of Bible College guidelines. After receiving candidate status (1976) and associate status (1978), Western was awarded full accreditation in 1980. At the graduation ceremony in April 1982, Western awarded Bachelor's degrees to qualifying graduates for the first time in its history.

During campus expansion in 1983, the municipality required that the College hook up its sewage disposal system to the municipal trunk line at the junction of Clayburn Road and No. 11 Highway. The line had to pass directly through the village of Clayburn. Although residents had the option of connecting their homes to the line, they chose not to participate. This may be the longest private sewer line in the municipality, extending 2.4 kilometres!

In October 1991, Western celebrated its 50th anniversary and contin-

WPBC graduates of 1991

Dr. James Richards, President

ues to develop its beautiful mountainside campus. For the last few years the average enrollment has been 215 students. By 1992, over 1300 graduates will have gone forth from the college. The majority of these now hold posts of responsibility as ministers, missionaries, church musicians, Christian educators, youth leaders, and trained lay persons within churches and church related institutions.

Western is proud to be a member of this municipality and congratulates Matsqui on the celebration of its 100th birthday.

Campus of Western Pentecostal Bible College, 35235 Straiton Road

58. Mennonite Central Committee (MCC)

For members of the Mennonite churches in British Columbia, service to needy people overseas goes hand-in-hand with service at home. MCC, an international organization, was created in 1920 in response to hunger and related human need brought on by war in the Soviet Union. In 1933, young people and their teachers in Yarrow raised money for MCC relief by growing beets and peas. In 1963 MCC Canada was created to coordinate Canadian relief and development efforts. MCC BC was formed October 24, 1964 as a charitable organization, to act as a united voice for Mennonite churches in B.C. Today approximately 1000 MCC personnel serve in assignments in 50 countries.

The Material Resources Warehouse at 31414 Marshall Road, Clearbrook serves as the storage, shipping and receiving center for western Canada. Volunteers pack donated articles such as soap, school kits, clothing and medical supplies for shipment overseas. Around 17,000 blankets and 4,800 layette bundles are processed annually.

Artisans in developing countries find employment through the sale of Selfhelp Crafts. Because the stores and special sale events are run by volunteers, overhead is low and the producers receive a reasonable income.

Thrift and Furniture Stores sell quality used items at reasonable prices in local communities. Income generated beyond expenses is used by MCC in developing countries.

The Refugee Assistance Program brings together people fleeing desperate situations and churches which offer a helping hand through sponsorship. Many refugees have been sponsored in B.C. during past years.

Funds for aid to developing countries are raised through annual Relief Sales. The sale and

Blankets being loaded into a container at the warehouse

Quilt auction at Relief Sale

auction of donated items such as hand-made quilts, crafts, baking and produce provide funds for the development work of MCC.

Jake Doerksen builds wooden toys for the Relief Sale

VOLUNTARY SERV-ICE places compassionate Christians where they can meet various human needs in B.C., elsewhere in Canada and around the world. Volunteers serve with Native people, as teachers, in housing projects, in counselling, with people who have disabilities, with single mothers, with refugee and family counselling, with care of the earth, with young offenders, with young people and with the elderly.

SUPPORTIVE CARE SERVICES began in 1974 with the creation of group home programs for people with mental handicaps. It nurtures people towards greater independence and responsibility in a supportive Christian environment.

EMPLOYMENT CONCERNS emerges out of MCC's long-standing commitment to development work with the poorest and weakest. Since 1990, MCC BC has applied overseas development skills locally, with refugee claimants and the mentally handicapped.

Through MENNONITE DISASTER SERVICE short-term volunteers help in areas devastated by natural disasters such as floods, earthquakes, hurricanes or tornadoes.

The NATIVE CONCERNS program places volunteers in northern native communities where they try to bring about healing and restoration of broken relationships. They encourage the resolution of justice issues involving native people and alert churches to those issues and needs.

SOCIAL HOUSING SOCIETY is a non-profit affiliate of MCC BC which provides affordable housing to needy persons in B.C. This enables people to make a home for themselves, and gives them hope for a better future.

The PEACE AND SERVICE COMMITTEE articulates the historic Mennonite conviction that Christ requires His followers to pursue non-violence and peacemaking. Its lecture series, seminars and other resources provide churches with information about peace, poverty, crime, capital punishment and other social concerns.

Through DEVELOPMENT EDUCATION MCC BC informs its supporters about poverty and challenges them to share in MCC development projects around the world.

MCC BC reports annually to the delegate body of the Mennonite churches of B.C. Between annual meetings, an elected executive committee supervises its operations. Administrative offices are located at 31872 South Fraser Way in Clearbrook.

Administrative Offices and Clothing Etcetera, Clearbrook Furniture, Roots Plus and Crafts of the World (Selfhelp) stores occupy the MCC Plaza opened in 1990.

59. Ebenezer Senior Home

Over the years we have often heard sermons on texts like "Love God above all and your neighbour as yourself" or "Honour your father and your mother." Putting these admonitions into practice takes action! In an attempt to do this, Rev. J. A. Botting, pastor of the First Christian Reformed Church of Vancouver, sponsored a meeting on January 22, 1964. He pointed out that the Fall 1963 CRC Diaconal Conference of Classis B.C., had recognized the need to provide a home for the aged. However, the conference could not be incorporated under the Societies Act of B.C. to be eligible for a grant in aid. Subsequently, Rev. Botting and the seven men present at that meeting set to work and on July 2, 1965, the Ebenezer Senior Home Society was registered in Victoria as a non-profit society.

The first public meeting was held on November 25, 1965 to stimulate a membership drive and to hear board members report on visits to Homes for the Aged which were for sale at that time. The drive brought the membership to 426. In spring, 1966, the CRC Church Classis B.C., recognized the Society as worthy of the spiritual and material support of the churches.

After two years of searching in vain for suitable property in the greater Vancouver area, property on Marshall Road in Abbotsford was

Ebenezer Home, 33433 Marshall Road

purchased. It was only three blocks from the First CR Church of Abbotsford.

On September 7, 1971 construction got under way for 16 self-contained units called "'tHofje" and 59 hostel units in the main building. The first 11 residents of the home and 8 tenants of the self-contained units moved in on August 31, 1972. One of the original residents, Mrs. H. Advocaat, still lives in the Home.

The official opening took place on September 16, 1972, with local, provincial and federal representatives in attendance. After thanksgiving to God, Ebenezer Society President Jack VanderVelden also thanked the many volunteers for their hard work on committees and organizations, which made this opening day possible.

Four administrators have guided the day to day operation of the Home: John Dykstra, August 1972 to July 1974; Ena Veeneman, July 1974 to April 1979; Coby Van Dam, April 1979 to August 1991; and Anne DeGraaff, the present matron, assisted by Jane Lammers, R.N. and 25 dedicated staff.

The Lord has graciously guided us through good times and bad. In the early days, the average age of the residents was between 65 and 70, and they participated in many activities. Today, the average age is 85 and the activities are of a different nature. However, the home-like atmosphere at Ebenezer remains its unique characteristic.

In February 1976, when fire broke out in the east wing, all the residents were led safely out of the building. It took two months to repair the damage. During a cold snap in February, 1989, an extended power outage resulted in frozen pipes, interior flooding and another evacuation. Many friends and family welcomed the elderly into their homes. Ten days

The Ebenezer inner court

Aerial view of Ebenezer Home complex

later, the residents moved "back home." In fall, 1990, a major face lift included installation of new windows, painting and replacing cedar shakes with metal.

The Ebenezer Home in the municipality of Matsqui is ideally suited for retirees and elderly persons who require assistance. The Board of Ebenezer Society has appointed an expansion committee which plans to utilize the rest of the Marshall Road property for high rise apartments and an intermediate care unit.

Ebenezer is still a private home, made possible by many hours of volunteer work and private donations. Over the last 20 years, many people have called Ebenezer "Home." We are indeed thankful to the Lord for allowing us to operate this facility for seniors. To all those who helped made it happen, a big "Thank you!"

60. The Mennonite Benevolent Society

In the early 1950's, a group of people became concerned about the welfare of our elderly people. On December 29, 1952, they organized the Mennonite Benevolent Society and registered it under the B.C. Societies Act. The objective of the Society was to provide a home that offered compassionate care to meet the needs of the elderly and ill people of the Mennonite faith.

The first project was the development of Menno Home, a rest home for the aged, dedicated and opened May 30, 1954. The need for a nursing home to care for the ill soon became apparent, and thus the Society constructed the Menno Private Hospital. This 36-

Menno Home, front entrance, 32910 Brundige

bed facility was opened in July 1960 as a private hospital (nursing home). In March 1965, a new wing added another 39 beds.

On December 11, 1965, Menno Private Hospital was designated as an extended care hospital under the B.C. Hospital Insurance Service department and the Hospital Act. The private hospital licence was recalled and the facility renamed Menno Hospital.

Its doors are open to anyone in the community, regardless of race, creed or religion. However, its objectives, philosophy and principles remain unchanged.

Menno Hospital, main entrance, 32945 Marshall Road

Today the Mennonite Benevolent Society offers care for the elderly on four specific levels:

1. Menno Hospital — extended care
2. Menno Home — intermediate care
3. Menno Pavilion — independent living.
4. Community Partnership Bathing Program

1. MENNO HOSPITAL — EXTENDED CARE

Menno Hospital provides the highest level of extended care services possible within the parameters of available resources. As of October, 1992, care will be provided to 150 residents, in an atmosphere of warmth and compassion, based on principles of Christian faith.

Care and service is offered by a multidisciplinary team of health care professionals with expertise in gerontology. The disciplines include nursing, physiotherapy, activities, pharmacy, medicine, dietetics and pastoral care.

The Pastoral Care department regularly interacts with community church groups to ensure continuity of spiritual care after admission.

2. MENNO HOME — INTERMEDIATE CARE

Care at the Menno Home, a 196-bed facility, is premised on belief in the dignity and worth of all elderly persons and in their right to an honourable, secure and comfortable life in a Christian caring environment.

Physiotherapy: Walking Program

Independence and active participation is encouraged. Services include room and board, daily personal and health care. An extensive program of social, spiritual and recreational activities are provided.

The Long Term Care Administrators/Assessors of the B.C. Ministry of Health control admission into Menno Home. While residential care is made available to society at large, many residents come with an ethnic Mennonite background.

The nursing staff provides 24-hour service. By assessing the resident's needs, planning, implementing and evaluating their nursing care, the staff supports optimal health.

Pastoral care by a full-time chaplain offers spiritual help to residents and their families. Services include Sunday worship, morning devotions and Bible studies.

The activity department gives residents opportunities to participate in various crafts, activities and outings.

The dietary department arranges for general and special nutritional needs.

3. MENNO PAVILION — INDEPENDENT LIVING

Sixty independent living units accommodate the elderly who are physically able to care for themselves. These units were intended primarily to house spouses of residents at Menno Hospital or Menno Home, but also provide affordable housing for other individuals or couples.

Services include: weekly monitoring by a registered nurse if desired; live-in caretaker services to assist in daily activities and in emergencies; Medi-Alert System that can be arranged at user expense; resident activities such as Bible studies and special programs, crafts and workshop, exercise classes and outings like bus trips. One meal a day is available Monday through Friday for a fee.

4. COMMUNITY PARTNERSHIP BATHING PROGRAM

The Mennonite Benevolent Society also supports the independence and well-being of elderly and disabled persons living in the community through its Bathing Program. Individuals who choose to remain in their homes despite physical limitations, may set up telephone appointments for baths to maintain personal hygiene.

Menno Pavilion

61. Tabor Home

Tabor Home, 31944 Sunrise Crescent, Clearbrook

Wherever Mennonites settled, they built institutions like churches and schools to accommodate the needs of their people. The Tabor Home came into being as the Mennonite Brethren response to the needs of their retired senior citizens in this area.

The care of the aged had always been regarded as the duty of children toward their parents. As the Psalm writer puts it, "Do not cast me off in time of old age; forsake me not when my strength is spent" (Ps. 71:9). During the days of the family farm, aging and infirm parents were usually cared for by the family until they passed away or, because of serious illness, had to be cared for in public or private hospitals. However, with

Mrs. Wittenberg in her room, 1963

179

changes in society, the need for a personal care home in the Matsqui area became apparent.

The Clearbrook MB Church, which had a large membership of senior citizens, proposed the construction of a Senior Citizens home to the MB Conference. But when the Conference did not accept that proposal, the Tabor Home Society was organized in September, 1959. Mennonite Brethren individuals, churches, women's clubs and Christian businesses became members. On July 18, 1960, sod was turned for the Tabor Home,

Administrator Friesen shaves blind Mr. Ediger, 1963

with accommodations for 39 residents. After prayerful consideration, Abe J. Friesen, a building contractor, together with his wife Katie, became the first houseparents. Within three weeks of opening on March 20, 1961, the Tabor Home reported full occupancy.

Meals are served in the dining hall

Only two years later, in 1963, the "East Wing" of 23 rooms was added. A growing waiting list of potential residents prompted plans for another addition which was completed in March, 1968, bringing the capacity of the Tabor Home to 90. An "addition to the addition" in 1970 made room for 101 residents.

From its beginning, residents at Tabor enjoyed Bible studies, Sunday morning services with special singing groups and ministers from local MB churches, and various programs including missionary reports. Men enjoyed activities like shuffleboard and table games, or walked to the Clearbrook shopping centres, weather and health permitting. Some of the ladies rolled bandages and engaged in crafts for MCC. Appealing, high quality meals occasionally have an ethnic flavour. All residents, including those in wheelchairs appreciated the beautiful grounds with flowers, an arbour, fish pond and fountain.

Since 1985, more than 50% of Tabor Home residents require Intermediate Care, rather than the lesser Personal Care. Presently, classification of "Intermediate Care I" is mandatory for admission. The staff includes an administrator and chaplain, nursing,

Thanksgiving service in the chapel

dietary, activity and maintenance personnel. The Tabor Home Society oversees the operation, which receives supplementary government funding.

In 1989, Sunset Manor, a three-storey apartment complex of independent living units, was constructed adjacent to Tabor. For a fee, its residents may elect to enjoy the noon meal (prepared at the Tabor kitchen), in their own spacious dining hall.

Tabor Home currently has 121 residents and operates a complete activity program emphasizing social, cultural and spiritual life as well as encouraging hobbies and crafts.

Aerial view of Tabor Home & Sunset Manor.

CONCLUSION

The rapid growth of population in this area and the parallel organiza-tion of some 75 congregations over the last century has also seen the establishment of a significant number of para-church organizations and church-related institutions. The Mennonite Central Committee, Conference of Mennonites in B.C., the B.C. Conference of Mennonite Brethren Churches and the Seventh Day Adventist Churches of B.C. and Yukon are among the groups with headquarters in this area. Campus Crusade and Youth for Christ also have branches here. Christian book-stores include Christian Book & Nutrition Centre, Derksen's Christian Supply, House of James and The Bookshelf. Stores like Bibles for Russia and MCC outlets raise money for Christian causes abroad. Other orga-nizations include Africa Evangelical Fellowship and Fraser Valley Senior Missionary Fellowship. Christian counselling centres include Burdenbearers and Columbia Christian Counselling group.

The Christian schools in the area were founded on the premise that "Christian education of the young is a must, not only in the home and church, but also in the day school." Our Christian colleges seek to "develop Christian character, application of biblical principles in all areas of life, lay a foundation for lifelong learning and equip students for prac-tical ministry in the church and in the world." The biblical injunction to "Honour your father and your mother," is being carried out in senior citi-zens homes that provide care "in an atmosphere of warmth and compas-sion, based on principles of Christian faith." Undergirding all these ministries, however, are the believers in the churches.

Today, in our area, "the gospel of love and reconciliation is being preached. The unchurched are finding a church home and a loving wel-come. Lives are being changed."

As Jake Tilitzky, moderator of the Conference of Mennonites, put it, "This historical account of the central Valley churches, published as part of Matsqui's Centennial celebrations, serves as a living testimonial to the trustworthiness of Christ's promise to His church. These churches and denominations, emphasizing various forms and traditions, portray the multifaceted redemptive mission of the church. The faithfulness of Christ to His church over the centuries encourages us to continue to be faithful as we move, not only into the next century, but on to the glorious fulfillment of the church's purpose in eternity."

These representative statements bear eloquent witness to the words of Jesus, "On this rock I will build my church and the gates of hell will not overcome it." Matthew 16:17

Select Bibliography

ANGLICAN

The Book of Alternative Services of the Anglican Church of Canada. Toronto: Anglican Book Centre, 1985.

The Book of Common Prayer. Toronto: Anglican Book Centre, 1962.

St. Matthew's Anglican Church 1900–1980. Abbotsford, B.C.: Parish of St. Matthew, 1980.

BAPTIST

BGC Canada News, Baptist General Conference of Canada, Edmonton, AB

Bergeson, John H. *The Fourth Quarter of the First Century: History of the Columbia Baptist Conference 1964–1989.* Columbia Baptist Conference, 1989.

Carlson, Gordon. *Seventy-Five Years of History of Columbia Baptist Conference, 1889–1964.* Seattle, WA: Columbia Baptist Conference, 1964.

CATHOLIC

Pax Regis. Biannual publication of Westminster Abbey and the Seminary of Christ the King, Mission, B.C.

The B.C. Catholic. Periodical. Vancouver, B.C.

Mission's Catholic Community and the Town That Grew Around it: St. Joseph's Parish: Golden Jubilee 1938–1988. Mission, B.C., 1988.

CHRISTIAN REFORMED CHURCH

Christian Reformed Church Yearbook. Published annually. Grand Rapids: CRC Board of Publications.

Doornbos, H., ed. *History of the Christian Reformed Community of Abbotsford, British Columbia.* Abbotsford, B.C.: Compiled & published by the local Christian Reformed Churches, 1991.

Kromminga, John. *In the Mirror: An Appraisal of the Christian Reformed Church.* Hamilton, Ontario: Guardian Press, 1957.

_____. *The Christian Reformed Church: A Study in Orthodoxy.* Grand Rapids: Baker Book House, 1949.

Van Dyk, Wilbert. *Belonging: An Introduction to the Faith and Life of the Christian Reformed Church.* Grand Rapids: CRC Publications, 1959.

Zwaanstra, Henry. *Reformed Thought and Experience in a New World.* Kampen: Kok. 1973.

EVANGELICAL BIBLE CHURCHES, FELLOWSHIP OF

Headquarters: 5800 South 14th Street, Omaha, Nebraska 68107 (402) 731–4780

Annual Report of the Fellowship of Evangelical Bible Churches. Omaha, Nebraska: Fellowship of Ev. Bible Churches. Published annually.

Frey, Robert L., ed. *Gospel Tidings.* Bi-monthly periodical. Omaha, Nebraska: Fellowship of Evangelical Bible Churches.

Wall, O. J. comp. *A Concise Record of our Evangelical Mennonite Brethren Annual Conference Reports 1889–1979.* Freeman, South Dakota: Pine Hill Press, n.d.

EVANGELICAL FREE

Hansen, Calvin B. *What It Means to be Free.* Minneapolis: Free Church
    Publications, 1990.

_____. *A Living Legacy: Essays on the Evangelical Free Church Movement,*
    Past, Present and Future. Compiled by the Spiritual Heritage
    Committee, Greg Scharf, chair. Minneapolis: Free Church
    Publication, 1990.

Hanson, Muriel. *Fifty Years and Seventy Places: the Evangelical Free Church in*
    Canada 1917–1967. Minneapolis: Free Church Publications, 1967.

LUTHERAN, EVANGELICAL

Tappert, Theodore G., ed. *The Book of Concord: the Confessions of the Evangelical*
    Lutheran Church. Philadelphia: Fortress Press, 1959.

Forell, George W. *The Augsburg Confession: a Contemporary Commentary.*
    Minneapolis: Augsburg Publishing House, 1968.

Vatja, Vilmos, etc. *The Lutheran Church Past and Present.* Minneapolis:
    Augsburg Publishing House, 1977.

Called to Be One: the Bulletin of Reports and Minutes of the Constituting
    Convention of the Evangelical Lutheran Church in Canada. Winnipeg,
    Manitoba, May 16–19, 1985.

Denef, Lawrence, trans. *Evangelical Catechism.* American Edition. Minneapolis:
    Augsburg Publishing House, 1982.

MENNONITES: CONFERENCE OF MENNONITES IN B.C.

Offices: 31414 Marshall Road, Clearbrook, B.C.

Eben-Ezer — 1963–1988. Abbotsford, B.C.: Eben-Ezer Mennonite Church,
    1988.

Loewen, David F. *Living Stones: A History of the West Abbotsford Mennonite*
    Church 1936–1986. Abbotsford, B.C.: West Abbotsford Mennonite
    Church, 1987.

The Mennonite Reporter. Conference of Mennonites periodical.
    Waterloo, ON.

MENNONITE BRETHREN

Mennonite Brethren Conference Office: 202–2464 Clearbrook Road,
Clearbrook, B.C.

Confession of Faith. Hillsboro, KS.: Board of Christian Literature, General
    Conference of Mennonite Brethren Churches, 1976.

Klassen, A. J. & Betty. *The King Road Mennonite Brethren Church: Highlights of*
    the First Twenty-Five Years (1966–1991). Abbotsford: King Road MB
    Church, 1991.

Mennonite Brethren Herald. Bi-monthly Canadian denominational periodical.
    Winnipeg, MB

Ratzlaff, Erich L. *The Clearbrook Mennonite Brethren Church (1936–1986).*
    Clearbrook: Clearbrook MB Church, 1986.

Schmidt, John P. "Pilgrims in Paradise: Sixty Years of Growth in the
    Mennonite Brethren Churches in British Columbia." Dissertation:
    Fuller Theological Seminary, 1991.

Stobbe, Abe J. *South Abbotsford Mennonite Brethren Church: A History from*
    1932–1982. Abbotsford: South Abbotsford MB Church, 1982.